WALK WITH ME

A BIBLICAL JOURNEY IN MAKING CHRISTLIKE DISCIPLES

HAL PERKINS

D0108944

BEACON HILL PRESS
OF KANSAS CITY

Copyright 2008 by Hal Perkins and Beacon Hill Press of Kansas City

ISBN 978-0-8341-2392-2

Printed in the
United States of America

Cover Design: Brandon Hill
Internal Design: Sharon Page

Library of Congress Cataloging-in-Publication Data

Perkins, Hal, 1945-
    Walk with me : a biblical journey in making Christlike disciples / Hal Perkins.
        p. cm.
    Includes bibliographical references.
    ISBN 978-0-8341-2392-2 (pbk.)
    1. Jesus Christ—Example. 2. Discipling (Christianity)—Biblical teaching. I. Title.

    BT304.2.P47 2009
    253—dc22

                                                                2008044385

10 9 8 7 6 5 4 3 2 1

To our favorite and best disciplemakers—David, Dana, Deborah, Daniel

Each of you has already surpassed your parents in ways never intended; not even imagined.

For you we had only one passion—to help you know and authentically follow Jesus.

We did not dream you would become preachers, teachers, authors, ministry-creators, and leaders.

We did try to help you become disciplemakers, and you have all surpassed our highest hopes.

How thankful we are to those who selected and discipled you far beyond what we could have.

Highest praise to Jesus for discipling you into Christlikeness and great fruitfulness.

And to Debbi—my precious partner and greatest human help

Without your faith in God and me . . .

Without your constant love and encouragement . . .

Without your partnering in ministry at home, in the church, and in the world . . .

Without your giving me freedom to follow my dream . . .

I am certain I would have caved in to all the pressures and given up on Jesus' clear call to me to make disciples.

CONTENTS

PREFACE

The ambitious aim of this book is to multiply Christlike disciplemakers. The realistic aim is to increase Christ-honoring conversations, commitments, and accountability to encourage modest progress in becoming more like Christ. The closer we are to what Christ was in love and practice, the more effectively He can work through us to build His Church (see Matt. 16:18; Heb. 12:14).

Many speak of discipleship. Usually they are speaking of only some—but not all—of the following five categories:

1. *Being discipled*—being personally discipled by God's Word, Spirit, and other Christians. We all need this help until our dying day (chaps. 1—2).

2. *Discipling others informally*—being Christlike wherever we are, including intentionally influencing non-Christians (chap. 5).

3. *Discipling other Christians toward maturity*—intentionally and strategically influencing Christians to know and follow Jesus (chaps. 6—11).

4. *Discipling maturing Christians to disciple (mentor) others* (chaps. 3, 4, 12).

5. *Discipling maturing Christian disciplers to intentionally help others in making Christlike disciples* (chap. 13).

Components 4 and 5 are the most challenging items in this list and are often omitted. Yet they are absolutely necessary to fulfill the Great Commission by multiplying leaders as Jesus intends.

In strategically making Christlike disciples, this book follows the steps outlined in Matt. 28:19-20:

Go, baptizing them in the name of the Father, Son, and Holy Spirit—Christlikeness everywhere (chap. 5).

Teaching—inviting others to willfully come under Jesus' influence (chap. 6).

To obey—helping those who respond to seek, trust, and serve Jesus (chaps. 7—10).

Everything—helping continuing responders with heart and life holiness (chap. 11), making Christlike disciples (chaps. 3, 4, 12), and making Christlike disciplemakers (chap. 13).

Jesus said His Father is always at work, and He, too, is working (John 5:17). We can be sure that Jesus is at work this very moment. But in many places where Christianity is culturally embraced, something—or someone—is not working as it should. Are the workers Jesus told His disciples to pray for (see Matt. 9:38) working too much at the things they *think* will work and not working enough at what Jesus *knows* will work?

For Christlike disciplemaking to multiply, we must establish significant intercessory prayer: "Holy Spirit, we desperately need Your help for us to 'be and do church' in very lost cultures—Your way. Please soften and enlighten our entrenched values, perspectives, and priorities."

We also must authentically model Christlikeness, including graciously helping others discover and follow Jesus. We must sensitively discover if others understand what it means to walk with Jesus. And then we must adopt, encourage, and help those who are interested in actually walking with Him.

I write not only as a lover of what Jesus loved and died for—His Church—but also as a grateful lover of my own denomination. My denomination's particular emphasis has led me to look long and hard at how it is we are to be holy—loving God entirely and becoming Christlike.

To protect identities, names in some stories have been changed. Some of the stories and concepts are fleshed out in much greater detail in my recently printed book, *If Jesus Were a Parent*.[1] That book is designed to help parents disciple their families. Because the family is the basic structure for close and lengthy relationships, and because close and lengthy relationships are needed to make disciples, well-discipled Christlike parents are our best hope for multiplying Christlike disciples.

1 — HOW DID JESUS WALK?

Whoever claims to live in him must walk as Jesus did *(1 John 2:6).*

Jesus said, "Follow me." First John 2:6 says that those claiming to live in Christ must walk as He walked. This book is about making Christlike disciples—getting and giving the help needed to walk the way Jesus walked. As we begin, may this prayer be on our lips: "Lord Jesus, please help us to know, love, and follow You better and to realize how much we need each other's help to become and make Christlike disciples."

What is a disciple?

Long ago a "maestro" or "master" would look for a student in whom to reproduce his expertise. To be selected, this student must demonstrate great potential. The master would then invite this student into an apprenticeship for a significant length of time. Through the influence of this relationship, the apprentice—or disciple—could watch, learn, be coached, and eventually duplicate the skills of the master.

But that was not all. The intent of the close and lengthy relationship was for the apprentice to absorb the passions, dreams, and secrets of the master. And the master continually observed the apprentice, always watching, always listening, to discover how well the apprentice was obtaining these things.

In this sense, we are all apprentices, disciples who live in close and lengthy relationships, being influenced by other people or things, for better and for worse. Family, school, coworkers, and the media have profoundly discipled us all. The issue is not *whether* anyone or anything is discipling us, but *who* or *what* is discipling us. Nor is the question, "Should I have a disciple?" The fact is, we *are* influencing—and thus discipling—others. The real issue is *how* we are discipling them.

To make Christlike disciples, we must be disciples— not of our culture—but of Christ

Fact: all of us *have been* discipled—profoundly influenced by someone or something—intentionally and unintentionally, formally and informally.

Fact: all of us *are being* discipled right now by every thought, word, sight, experience, and relationship that influences us.

Fact: all of us *are making* disciples—influencing others based on precisely who and what we are—to varying degrees.

But God, through His Spirit, is also influencing every Christian and every lost person (see John 16:7-15). His gracious truth comes to us all, whether or not we believe in Christ, as an encouraging or convicting influence (see Rom. 8:9; John 16:7-15). The battle for the heart of every person's eternal destiny boils down to influence and how he or she responds to that influence.

We cannot help being discipled—influenced—by all that surrounds us. However, we can intentionally and proactively seek to know and follow a mentor, a coach, a good father or mother.

To purposely attach ourselves to someone in order to follow him or her is the essence of *intentionally* being discipled.

Why can it realistically be said that all of us have been and are being discipled? That all of us are making disciples?

Even Jesus was influenced. He purposely and proactively attached himself to His Father (see Luke 4:42; 5:16; 6:12; 21:37; 22:39, 41). In intriguing ways, His relationship with His Father is like that of a disciple with a mentor. It's a helpful model for us to better understand what it means to become and make Christlike disciples.

What is a disciple of Jesus?

A disciple of Jesus knows and follows Him. He or she walks *with* Jesus for a lifetime.

- "Come to me" (Matt. 11:28).
- "Follow me" (Matt. 16:24).
- "This is how we know we are in him: Whoever claims to live in him must walk as Jesus did" (1 John 2:5-6).

Disciples of Jesus increasingly walk *as* Jesus walked.

What do Jesus' disciples learn as they watch and listen to Jesus?

First, they come to realize the intentionality and impact of Jesus' relationship with His Father.

First John 2:3-6 affirms that every Christian is to walk as Jesus walked. So how did Jesus walk? As we will soon discover, Jesus walked in a close, sensitive relationship with His Father.

Jesus says to us, "Follow me." So following Jesus, walking as He walked, begins by walking in a close, sensitive relationship with our eternal Father.

Further, when Jesus made disciples, He did not organize a

seminar or teach through a systematic curriculum. He invited twelve young men to walk with Him. They spent much time with Him—in a close and lengthy relationship. They walked, served, and ate together. They *dialogued* many times with Him about what mattered most:

- Jesus' Father
- Jesus himself
- The kingdom of God
- Jesus' disciples, their understanding of the issues and their response to them

Finally, when Jesus directed His disciples to make disciples (Matt. 28:16-20), they automatically assumed He was calling them to do with others what He had done with them. They were to say to a few, "Walk with me"; that is, bring others into a close and lengthy relationship—walking, serving, eating—all the while dialoguing with them about what matters most. It never entered their minds that making disciples might mean teaching a seminar or studying through a curriculum, good and valuable as seminars and curricula are. (We must provide emerging leaders with a biblical track to run on, while not omitting long-term relational coaching.)

Why do you think Jesus gave so much of himself to just a few called His disciples? When He directed His disciples to make disciples, what do you think they imagined themselves doing to make disciples?

Based on their experience with Him, Jesus' disciples could only conclude that His commission to make disciples (see Matt. 28:18-20) was mostly about making close, meaningful, lengthy relationships.

Let's take a closer look at the Person at the center of what making disciples is all about: Jesus.

Jesus' time with His Father

Jesus' relationship with His Father is the closest and most meaningful relationship there could be. This is abundantly clear when we consider several important features of this relationship that we should follow.

First, Jesus intentionally gave himself to consistent and intensive amounts of time to be with His Father.

- "At daybreak Jesus went out to a solitary place" (Luke 4:42).
- "But Jesus often withdrew to lonely places and prayed" (Luke 5:16).
- "One of those days Jesus went out to a mountainside to pray, and spent the night praying to God" (Luke 6:12).
- "Each evening he went out to spend the night on the hill called the Mount of Olives" (Luke 21:37).
- "Jesus went out as usual to the Mount of Olives . . . and prayed" (Luke 22:39, 41).

Jesus loved His Father and loved being with Him, even when it was costly to His physical needs, other relationships, and tasks. He only had three years to accomplish His mission, yet He set aside vast amounts of time to dialogue with His Father. The One Person who often is assumed to least need any kind of help seemed to be the One who sought His Father's help the most.

Think about the passion Jesus had for His relationship with His Father and your lifestyle as His follower.

- How much do you think Jesus enjoyed getting alone with His Father?
- What other reasons might there be for Him to spend so much time with His Father?

- Since Jesus spent much time alone with His Father, and we are His followers, how important is it for us to set aside time to be with our Father?
- In light of our needs, time pressures, and global mission, what can Jesus' followers do to sustain the kind of "Father focus" that Jesus did?
- How much do you enjoy getting alone with your Heavenly Father?
- How do you evaluate the times you have with Him?
- How much help do you need from other disciples of Jesus to sustain time with your Father?

If we desire to be Christlike, we must begin by setting aside a substantial amount of time to spend in relationship with our Heavenly Father.

Jesus did only His Father's will

A second characteristic of Jesus' relationship with His Father that we seek to follow is Jesus' absolute determination to discern and do only what His Father was doing. His *actions* were a copy of what He observed in His Father.

- "I tell you the truth, the Son can do nothing by himself; he can do only what he sees his Father doing, because whatever the Father does the Son also does" (John 5:19).
- Speaking of His Father, Jesus says, "I always do what pleases him" (John 8:29).
- "The world must learn that I love the Father and that I do exactly what my Father has commanded me" (John 14:31).

Notice the relational component Jesus speaks of: He watches His Father and then does what He sees His Father doing. Jesus didn't lack the ability to act independently; He just wouldn't allow himself to act independently of His Father. Because of Jesus' love for His Father and absolute loyalty to Him, Jesus looked to

His Father for direction in all He did.

Think about everything we know Jesus did, such as going to Cana or Jerusalem, walking on water, or providing food for multitudes. Every single act was the direct result of Jesus' discerning His Father's will. Astonishing! What love for His Father! (see John 14:31).

Jesus' relationship with His Father models the ideal He intends for us as His disciples and for those we disciple: We are to watch and follow Him just as He watched and followed His Father, and we are to help those we are discipling to watch and follow Him as He followed His Father (chaps. 6—13).

Jesus said, "Follow me." If, for whatever reasons, He would not allow himself to do anything on His own but only did what He first saw His Father doing, how intentionally must we, as His disciples, learn to watch Him before we act? How much help will you need from fellow disciples to obey at this level? How much must we help those we coach in following Jesus to slow down and attempt to find out what Jesus is doing before acting?

Jesus judged only as His Father judged

A third characteristic of Jesus' relationship with His Father is that Jesus did not come to any *judgments* (conclusions) on His own. He had His own thoughts and was tempted to rely on His human understanding (see Heb. 4:15; Matt. 4:1-11; Prov. 3:5-6), but He passed each test by carefully submitting to the conclusions of His Father. "By myself I can do nothing; I judge only as I hear, and my judgment is just, for I seek not to please myself but him who sent me" (John 5:30).

Jesus was so sensitive to His Father that although He was

How does knowing that Jesus refused to come to conclusions independently of His Father make you feel about Him? Do you desire to walk in this way? How much help will you need to walk as Jesus walked, especially when it comes to making judgments (conclusions) about people and circumstances? Where could you get this kind of help? Can you help others to walk as Jesus walked in this way? How?

tempted just as we are, He brought all His thoughts (before they became independent, unilateral judgments or conclusions) into the light before they lodged in His mind. (Note 2 Cor. 10:5.)

Think about all the encounters Jesus had with people: Pharisees, prostitutes, tax collectors, proud and selfish disciples. Never once did He make a judgment about any of them apart from discerning His Father's thoughts and agreeing with His Father.

Again, Jesus supremely demonstrates how we are to be His disciples and to help others be His disciples. To follow Him, we must determine to relate to our Father as He did. To do this, we must do all we can to find out His judgment concerning any person or situation. We, and those we disciple, need much help to walk as Jesus walked (1 John 2:3-6; chaps. 6—13).

Jesus spoke only as His Father spoke

The fourth characteristic of Jesus' relationship with His Father is this: After He had sensitively been with and listened to His Father, Jesus *said* nothing other than what He heard His Father guiding Him to say.

- "I do nothing on my own but speak just what the Father has taught me" (John 8:28).

- "For I did not speak of my own accord, but the Father who sent me commanded me what to say and how to say it. . . . So whatever I say is just what the Father has told me to say" (John 12:49-50).
- "The words I say to you are not just my own. Rather, it is the Father, living in me, who is doing his work" (John 14:10).

Can you imagine never speaking until you have conversed with your Heavenly Father to be sure it is what He wants said? This is precisely what Jesus did. Standing before Pilate, judged wrongly by Pharisees, mocked by even His own brothers, Jesus refrained from responding until He knew what His Father wanted Him to say.

Through His intentional relationship with His Father, Jesus spoke only words given Him by His Father. In so doing, He models for us how we ought to follow Him as His disciples: We are to *secure all the help needed* to say only what He is intending to say through us. To do this, I need not only the Holy Spirit and the Scriptures but also the company of others who are growing as Jesus' disciples.

How much does meditating on Jesus' relationship with His Father strengthen your admiration for Jesus? Why? What do you think about walking as He walked? How much help will you need to make serious progress in walking as Jesus walked? To whom might you say, "Please walk with me. I need help to walk as Jesus walked"? What do you think about prayerfully adopting a few others to help them be Jesus' disciples? (see Mark 3:14).

Moreover, we must sufficiently relate to those we are discipling so that they can also walk as Jesus walked and be in such a consistent and close relationship to their Father that their words become increasingly God's words (chaps. 6—13).

In the next chapter, we will observe what may have been the all-time best example of an effective discipling conversation.

▶ **My Thoughts**

_____

_____

_____

_____

_____

_____

_____

_____

_____

_____

_____

_____

_____

_____

_____

2 --- HISTORY'S MOST EMPOWERING RELATIONSHIP

My Father, if it is not possible for this cup to be taken away
unless I drink it, may your will be done *(Matt. 26:42)*.

My prayer for this chapter is that all of us—especially leaders—will receive greater insight into who or what is currently discipling us. I also pray that we will increase in our love for Jesus and eagerly seek more help from our fellow Christ-followers in being Christlike.

As we observed in chapter 1, to be Jesus' disciples and to help others be His disciples, we must learn to walk as He walked. The foremost characteristic of Jesus' walk was His relationship with His Father, which included

- spending a large amount of quality time alone with His Father
- doing only what He observed His Father doing

- coming to conclusions only through consultation with His Father
- speaking only what He heard His Father guiding Him to speak

In this chapter, we will look closely at one of Jesus' many meetings with His Father. This meeting illustrates nicely the kind of meetings wise parents have with children, mentors have with learners, and disciplemakers have with disciples.

Discipling at its best

One night Jesus met with His Father in the Garden of Gethsemane. In this meeting we find portrayed grace and truth and the resulting Kingdom-empowering influence found in dynamic discipling at its best.

> During the days of Jesus' life on earth, he offered up prayers and petitions with loud cries and tears to the one who could save him from death, and he was heard because of his reverent submission. Although he was a son, he learned obedience from what he suffered *(Heb. 5:7-8)*.

In preparation for the most difficult experience of His life, Jesus returned to the garden to meet with His Father in prayer. He had had countless meetings alone with His Father. In those meetings, the human Jesus knew His Heavenly Father as Mentor, Discipler, Encourager, and Strengthener.

In the garden, God the Father patiently listened to His Son and remarkably influenced Him: "Jesus went out as usual to the Mount of Olives, . . . knelt down and prayed" (Luke 22:39, 41). Jesus experienced such anguish that His sweat was like drops of blood. What intense mental turmoil could cause this?

Three hours of intense, agonizing prayer passed (see Matt. 26:36-44). Jesus' bloodlike sweat and anguish were replaced with holy, courageous obedience that embraced the Cross. He went into the garden distraught. He came out with His face set like stone. What happened? What changed? We know three things for sure:

- Overwhelmed to the point of death, the Son of God had poured out His heart to His Father.
- His wise Father had patiently listened and compassionately responded.
- The Son was somehow strengthened in His resolve to embrace the Cross.

When a human father or mentor or spiritual coach listens and compassionately responds so that God's will is done, it is discipling at its best.

As Jesus' disciples, we daily take up our cross to follow Him. This routinely includes laying down our lives to help others. And this often leads to significant emotional pain. Though our anguish may not equal what Jesus experienced, we often long for someone to whom we can pour out our hearts the way Jesus did to His Father. We know we can approach our Heavenly Father with our burdens and joys, but sometimes we need a human mentor to hear and guide us. Do you have someone to listen who cares and will help you discern the Father's point of view?

On this night, Jesus returned one more time to the garden where He so often had met with His Father. There, as had happened so many times, Jesus was strengthened by His Father. Was it a reminder of His Father's love? His support? His perspective? The purpose of the Cross? Whatever Jesus received from His Father, it rekindled His passion and renewed His resolve to carry out His mission.

Jesus' anticipation of the Cross could generate every dreadful emotion known to any fully-human being. Perhaps He had seen a Roman crucifixion. He knew the Cross was the plan He and His Father had shared since before the foundation of the world. He understood He would be suffering on behalf of all people for every sin ever committed, past or future. And now He surely sensed the agony of what He would experience.

Although we do not know exactly what Jesus anticipated or experienced, we do know that the One who calmly informed Pilate that no power on earth could hurt God's Son unless it was the will of the Father, now had sweat pouring from His body like great drops of blood. In anguish, He fell on His face, crying out to His Father, "Father, if you are willing, take this cup from me" (Luke 22:42).

As Christians, we are firmly convinced that Jesus was fully God (see John 1:1-5; Phil. 2:6; Col. 1:15-20; Heb. 1:1-4). We also understand that Jesus was fully human.

What do you think Jesus, the incarnate Word, was experiencing when He was in so much anguish that His soul was "overwhelmed with sorrow to the point of death"? (Matt. 26:38; Luke 22:42). What do you think happened in the garden that led Jesus from "Father, if you are willing, take this cup from me" to "not my will, but yours be done"?

Meditate with me long and hard about Jesus' human mental state. He was in such a condition that He actually asked His Father to consider possibilities other than the Cross. Think about Jesus in such mental turmoil and emotional pain that His sweat was like drops of blood. How did Jesus, being all that He was, become so troubled?

A personal, life-transforming encounter

One night while in college, I was meditating on Jesus' experience in the garden. As I meditated, I became aware of the Father responding to Jesus' request. I didn't purposely create the following scenario. I simply saw it happen in my mind. I wouldn't claim with complete certainty that the conversation I observed was inspired, but I think it was. I do know that the Holy Spirit has used that experience to create a purifying passion in my heart that has dramatically shaped my entire life.

In my heart, I sensed that Jesus was desperate. He looked up to His Father and said, "Father, do I have to do this?" and then there was silence. The Gospels record that Jesus prayed three times over what appears to be three long hours. (I can't imagine Him not repeating His request over and over. When desperate, I pray that way too.) So He prays once more, "Do I have to go to the Cross?" Then silence. He prays again, "Is there any other way that We can get this done?"

> Do you have a mentor who asks you questions about your ideas? About your knowledge of the Scriptures and theology? About your God-dreams and plans to serve Jesus?

The Son is gently coached by the Father

I sensed God the Father speaking to Jesus. "Oh, My Son," He seemed to say, "With You I am infinitely pleased (Matt. 3:17). You have fulfilled Your mission perfectly. You sacrificed all of Your privileges and powers as God (Phil. 2:5-9). You were made like Your brothers in every way (Heb. 2:17). You were tempted more than any person ever has been (4:15). You were dramatically tempted to use Your relationship with Me to Your advantage, yet You would not (Matt. 4:1-10). You have been perfect. Oh, that You could feel the depths of My joy and delight in You!" (Matt. 3:17; 17:5). Into Jesus' heart, filled with dread, His Father pours heart-renewing, energy-generating truth.

This is precisely the kind of truth that good fathers pour into their children's anguished hearts, that good Sunday School teachers pour into the hearts of the Christ-followers they mentor. What is needed? A Christ-focused, caring, honest relationship.

As I meditated that night and the scene continued to unfold in my mind, I heard the Father continue to gently, compassionately whisper into His beloved Son's pained soul: "I see those who have given over their hearts to evil to plot against You. But, Son, remember that as I love You, I love them. Though I do not want You to suffer temporarily, I do not want them to suffer eternally. I want them to be with Us forever (2 Pet. 3:9). I love You and am delighted with You; I love them, and My heart is broken for them. How delighted I would be if they would change their minds about Us. How I long for them to relate to Me from their hearts."

Did Jesus have a choice? What kind of choices must disciples make? How can a mentor help a disciple make the best choices?

I could just picture Jesus' Father, after listening to the pain-filled heart of His Son for three hours, now sensitively filling His Son's poured-out heart with a Father's thoughts. Though not as intense, I personally believe this kind of dialogue happened routinely when Jesus was alone with His Father.

Even if this is not exactly what happened, this is how good disciplemakers help their disciples: they question their disciples about their thoughts, emotions, and desires. They listen for, or carefully ask their disciples about, the Father's perspective. Then they graciously offer their own understanding of the Father's perspective before asking their disciples what they conclude the Father's desire might be.

That night I envisioned Jesus' Father influencing His Son by helping Him see again images of the vision they shared and affirming Jesus as He faces the Cross: "My Son, I hear Your cries and so desire to deliver You. Oh, how I ache for You! This will be terrible for both of Us, but Your blood will become the blood of a new covenant that will allow all people, regardless of their sins, to be fully and freely forgiven and enter into a relationship with Us. I love You. I love the world. But You are free to choose."

It is one thing to make a request of a father and for the father to make the decision. It is another thing for a father, in love and wisdom, to give a hard choice back to a son.

I continued to meditate on this imagined, unfolding Father-Son conversation. I envisioned Jesus looking to the Cross and shuddering. He looked upward at His Father and felt loved and valued. How He loved His Father.

He observed His disciples sleeping despite His plea for support. He looked again at the Cross. He mentally anticipated His arrest and trial. Again, the anticipation of the Cross generated bloodlike sweat.

As He lingered in His Father's presence, compassion for His disciples and His enemies—for every person's eternal well-being—flowed through His Spirit-aided heart (Luke 4:1, 14, 18; Matt. 12:28; Acts

Do you have a Christ-following mentor you consistently meet with for "heart checks"? Can you confess your darkest motives, greatest fears, deepest pain?

10:38). He looked forward to the millions, possibly billions, of redeemed ones. Now He himself could envision them joyfully singing and dancing, experiencing His Father's goodness and glory. They were His eternal Bride— holy, like Him, perfected in unity.

Gradually, the emotional pain subsided. No more shuddering. The bloodlike sweat began to dry. No longer did Jesus pray, "Let this cup pass from me." Now, with Spirit-strengthened resolve, Jesus spoke what I believe to be the greatest words ever uttered, "Not my will, but yours be done."

This is the kind of conversation disciples need—not just once in a while—but routinely. Our "little" crosses confuse us, discourage us, and mitigate against the truth that "just yesterday" stirred us with passion, purpose, and boldness. Left untended, little by little, the darkness sets in, lies replace truth, and "nominal Christianity" replaces authentic Christ-following.

The perfectly wise Father only influenced—did not control—His Son in this crucial moment. Result: Jesus saw and chose His Father's will.[1]

Our Heavenly Father has declared that we are free. We have no choice but to make choices. If Jesus had no choice, He would not have been like us nor would He have represented us. Based on what we know about Jesus' relationship with His Father (chap. 1), I believe that in Jesus' hours of supreme need, He

> What is the quality of the meetings you have with your mentor? How consistent are they? How much do you talk about your behavior in the light of Jesus' example? About your attitudes and motives? About Jesus' dream and plan for your coming days?

poured out His heart to His listening Father. In response, His Father planted good seed into an open heart and reinforced the Son's determination to complete His mission.

Jesus and His Father had met many times before this greatest-of-all meeting, and repetitious meetings like those Jesus had with His Father greatly increase Christlikeness in contemporary disciples. As mentioned earlier, these purposeful meetings are the primary strategies for intentionally becoming and making disciples (chaps. 6—13). Through these meetings spiritual fathers and mothers can partner with spiritual sons and daughters to discover and mutually commit to God's highest will.

The discipling conversation that shaped eternity

Jesus began His Gethsemane prayer time in agony; He finished with clarity. What happened? What brought about this change? Jesus had an open-hearted conversation with His Father that strengthened His vision, passion, and resolve.

How much passion for Jesus will you need to persist in being mentored? In discipling a few others? How well are you being mentored in your place of prayer by the Word? How well do you bring your motives and thoughts to the Holy Spirit for dialogue? How are you preparing to be a Christ-following mentor—not controller—who listens as your disciples pour out their hearts?

I wonder if you feel what I feel as I write this? Do you feel the heart of the Father for Jesus? Do you feel the Father's heart for all of us? Can you imagine the tearing and ripping in His heart as He simultaneously observed Jesus' pain and our need?

Do you feel Jesus' heart for His Father? Do you feel

Jesus' heart for us? Do you feel the terrible tension of His heart, ripped apart by the agonizing decision? Torn by dread of the ultimate suffering on one side and profound love for His Father and us on the other? I feel it in both Father and Son. It ignites profound amazement and love in me for my Heavenly Father! It ignites unspeakable passion for my Lord and Savior, Jesus Christ.

So now Jesus invites us to be involved in the eternal mission that He and His Father share. When we realize the cost and ask Him if we must sacrifice, even suffer, He meets us in our Gethsemane and helps us see the eternal benefits to everyone involved. There He helps us say, "Not my will, but yours be done."

The prayer for the next two chapters is that each of us will see why Jesus calls us to intentionally make disciples, and that each of us will be convicted by the Holy Spirit to take the next steps in becoming disciplemakers.

▶ **My Thoughts**

3 — MAKING THE MOST WITH LESS

"Come, follow me," Jesus said *(Matt. 4:19)*.

To make Christlike disciples, we need the revelation of Jesus' ministry

On July 4, 1969, my life was changed forever.

The preceding November, Debbi and I had announced our engagement. I had just completed my first year as a math teacher and third as varsity basketball coach. On July 4, 1969, exactly one month and five days before we were to be married, Debbi and I decided to attend the annual July 4th family camp near Spokane, Washington, where she lived.

On that day, we attended the church service. As I listened to the message, the Holy Spirit overwhelmed me with a call into pastoral ministry. To this day I believe it was God's voice I heard. After the service, Debbi and I went for a walk. We talked meaningfully about my sense that God was calling me to become a pastor. I had already signed a contract to teach and coach the following year. We determined to pray during the year, and if I still believed the Lord had called me to change professions, we would do so. After another year of teaching and coaching, I still felt the same. The result: our lives were changed forever.

I was actually fearful of becoming a pastor. Having grown up in a small church, I had watched and heard about the challenges. I decided that if I were called to be a pastor, my best hope for fruitfulness would be to study Jesus' life and ministry for how He might pastor.

I intensely studied all four Gospels. My intent was to learn all that I could from Jesus and, as much as possible, let His ministry pattern be my ministry pattern.

I observed the Bible's depiction of Jesus' preaching ministry to the masses. I noted His care for the temporary needs of people. In the midst of all this, a surprising theme emerged: Jesus spent a great amount of time with a very small group of His followers who later became leaders in His world-changing mission. When Jesus preached to the masses, helped the hurting, spent time with the lost, or battled with religious leaders, a few men were almost always with Him. Toward the end of His time on earth, Jesus spent most of His time with this small group. They were called His disciples. They became His family (Matt. 12:48-50). Through them, Jesus "turned the world upside down" (Acts 17:6, KJV).

I believe that if Jesus were to be a pastor today, among all His other responsibilities, He would prioritize making disciples. In the midst of other pastoral activity, if I really trusted Jesus enough to follow Him (that is what Christians do), an essential component in pastoring would be making disciples.

As clearly as the Holy Spirit called me into professional

ministry, He equally called me to make disciplemaking a priority of ministry. I have, at times, focused on disciplemaking with such intensity that people thought I knew nothing else. In other seasons of ministry, I have neglected intentional disciplemaking, for which I have repented.

After studying all the Gospels and concluding that Jesus would prioritize disciplemaking, I launched into another intensive study of the Gospels. This time my goal was to discover, if possible, exactly how Jesus made disciples. You will see the impact of that study throughout the course of this book. For now, the point of supreme importance is that Jesus invested great amounts of time in making disciples.

Doesn't it seem illogical that Jesus would so seriously give himself to disciple so few people?

> How much time and emphasis do you think Jesus gave to making disciples? What are your conclusions about why He strategically invested so much in so few? As His follower, how has the fact that He invested so much in so few impacted what you do with your family and church?

What did Jesus know?

Jesus came to save the world (John 3:17). He came to seek and to save the lost (Luke 19:10). To seek and to save the lost is an enormous mission, an unthinkable job description. Was Jesus truly strategic in determining to "focus on the few" in order to achieve His Father-ordained mission? Would Jesus really invest huge amounts of time hanging out with a few young, untested, passionate fisherman types? Why did that which is nonsense to us make such sense to Him?

I believe He knew that holy, strategic leaders would be absolutely necessary to move His vision and ministry forward, and that this would not occur without intense personal relationship and mentoring. Perhaps He knew that it is difficult to sustain long-term the laying down of one's life for God without caring friends and spiritual coaching. Perhaps He understood that quantity is the by-product of quality, and to produce quality in people demands great personal attention. Maybe He knew how much personal attention is required to simply believe, repent, and follow an invisible Lord and Savior. Perhaps His theology was more about how we finish the race than how we start it. Whatever it is that He knew, for some reason or reasons, He focused on the few to reach the masses.

Here is something Jesus knew that we must grasp: the vast majority of Christians—there are certainly exceptions—will not mature in Christlikeness nor make Christlike disciples without being intentionally and intensively discipled. Standing in worship services, sitting through sermons and other forms of one-way communication, reading books, and then going it alone has not and will not result in nearly enough Christlike disciples and disciplemakers. Almost all of us need intentional, intensive, fairly long-term relationships with mentors who are effectively following Jesus and know good ways to help us follow Him.

Many invited; a few chosen

Jesus invited all to come and learn of Him (Matt. 11:28-29), but not without clearly explaining the cost involved.

- If you follow Me, you may not have a place to sleep at night and you may not have time for things others assume to be important (8:18-22).
- Your loyalty to Me will cause conflict even with family members who want you to go along with them instead of

following Me. If you love them more than Me, you are not worthy of Me. If you don't say no even to yourself in order to say yes to Me, you are not worthy of Me (10:37-39).

• To a rich young man who was seriously seeking eternal life, Jesus said, "If you want to be perfect, go, sell your possessions and give to the poor, and you will have treasure in heaven. Then come, follow me" (19:21).

Sometime after many were sufficiently intrigued with Jesus to follow Him, He stayed up all night in prayer. The reason: He was conversing with His Father about who He should select to personally disciple (Luke 6:12-13). These He intentionally invited into close, personal relationship (Mark 3:13-14).

First, He invited everyone. Then, He told them the cost. Then, He selected twelve to be with Him.

Selecting disciples

Many challenges exist for us in selecting disciples to invest in. There is no question about our first choice. It is our family members, especially those still in our home or geographical vicinity.

Beyond family, we intentionally serve people from our church and our world in order to begin the disciplemaking process (chap. 5). This opens doors to invite those served to learn of Jesus together (Matt. 11:28-29; Luke 6:17). The best way to begin involving others in formal disciplemaking is an open group, to which the intentional disciplemaker invites everyone possible (chap. 6). From those who respond, you set in motion processes whereby the disciplemakers help disciples grow in Christlikeness (chaps. 7—11). Mentors then call disciples to make disciples themselves. Those who respond are selected to be intensively discipled, including being in a group for mentors, for as long as helpful for fruitfulness (chaps. 12—13).

I believe that Jesus' first priority was His relationship with His Father (chaps. 1—2). After that, I believe Jesus' second priority was to invest enormous amounts of His limited time in a carefully chosen few—His disciples who were like His family (Matt. 12:49). To be sure, there were many other things He did, but not to the exclusion of His first two priorities.

Demonstrating ministry

As I researched my way through the Gospels, I was dramatically impressed with how much Jesus ministered.[1] Much of the Gospel story is the record of Jesus simply doing good (Acts 10:37-38).

It was somewhere in this process that it dawned on me that much of the time that Jesus was doing all this ministry, His disciples were hanging around watching Him (Mark 5:35-43). These themes—personal ministry and discipling others for ministry—are the topics of chapters 5 and 10.

Many of the recorded times that Jesus taught, His disciples were "in the meeting."[2] Routinely, the disciples and Jesus discussed the issues He had just taught, in "the meeting after the meeting."[3] The disciples participated in some of Jesus' many prayer meetings.[4]

Teaching and supervising ministry

He also, almost classroom style, gave them a lot of instruction before sending them out into ministry (Matt. 10; Mark 6:7-11). He then officially sent them out to practice ministry. When they came back, He had them give accounts of their experiences in ministry (v. 30; Luke 9:10; 10:17). We will study this process in chapter 6.

With Him

Jesus' disciples had amazing access to Him. Notice how persistently they came to Him for direction (Mark 3:14; Acts 4:13).

- "The disciples came to him and asked, 'Why . . . ?'" (Matt. 13:10).
- "His disciples came to him and said, 'Explain . . .'" (v. 36).
- "As evening approached, the disciples came to him and said . . ." (14:15).
- "'Lord, if it's you,' Peter replied, 'tell me to come to you on the water'" (v. 28).
- "Then the disciples came to him and asked . . ." (15:12).
- "So his disciples came to him and urged him . . ." (v. 23).
- "At that time the disciples came to Jesus and asked . . ." (18:1).
- "Then Peter came to Jesus and asked . . ." (v. 21).
- "Jesus left the temple and was walking away when his disciples came up to him to call his attention to its buildings" (24:1).
- "As Jesus was sitting on the Mount of Olives, the disciples came to him privately" (v. 3).
- "On the first day of the Feast of Unleavened Bread, the disciples came to Jesus and asked . . ." (26:17).

Focus on the few

This amazing availability of Jesus to a few, resulting in life-transforming observations and conversations, could not occur for thousands or hundreds or even dozens of people. Time and energy are limited. Jesus determined it better to train a few deeply and miss other opportunities than to train many in just a superficial education.

The Bible records numerous instances of Jesus simply being

with His disciples: "road trips,"[5] meals,[6] special events,[7] and retreats.[8] It was in these casual, unguarded times of being together, where life erupted and hearts were opened, that Jesus greatly shaped the disciples.[9] These informal but intentional times of disciplemaking are the most needed and least practiced parts in most discipling models today. Here the skilled mentor makes the life and heart of the disciple his or her curriculum for study. The mentor watches, asks, listens, then strategically brings Jesus' grace and truth into a life-related, open, teachable heart. This is the issue of chapters 8—9, methodologically the most important chapters of the book.

Everyone needs a Jesus in the flesh

Jesus' disciples needed access to Him just as a child needs his or her parents.

I need this kind of access to Jesus. I have it by way of the Holy Spirit, whom Jesus guaranteed would guide me into all truth (John 16:13). Further, I have the Bible, God's written words and love letter to me. However, I truly need Jesus in the flesh to help me. I need someone to dialogue with me about Jesus, His Word, His will, my blind spots, ideas, attitudes, motives, emotions, reactions, truth, faith, love, success, pride, fear, failures, questions, confusion, discouragement, and so on. I need mature disciples of Jesus who know me well, love me anyhow, and care enough to help me know and follow Jesus. If you cannot find a Christlike mentor, don't wait. Invite some peers or even less mature persons to partner with you in helping each other know and follow Jesus (chap. 6).

Debbi and I committed to private times every week to listen to and disciple each of our children. From those purposeful, consistent conversations that brought life's events to Jesus for Truth, we talked much more naturally about Jesus in the routine and challenges of everyday life.

One day, our daughter Dana greatly needed access to someone who would be Jesus in the flesh. She later recorded the moment.

I remember sitting in the specialist's office at the age of nine when I was diagnosed with an autoimmune disease called polyarteritis nodosa. It was one of the scariest moments in my little life thus far. Immediately the flood of accusations came against me—that I would never be normal, that I would always be different because I was sick. Later on that day as my triplet brother and sister asked me about the doctor's appointment, I suddenly felt so different than them, so separate and alone. Overwhelmed, I burst into tears and ran inside. There my father embraced me in my tears and took me upstairs to talk about what I was feeling. Little did I know all that he must have been feeling as a father, aching over the pain of the difficult diagnosis given to his daughter, asking the Lord his own questions and experiencing his own inward wrestlings. Yet he did not treat this more challenging time any differently than all the ordinary times, but rather began to ask me the familiar questions that I knew so well, leading my heart back into truth. He began to tell me that Jesus was giving me an invitation right now—He wanted to invite me to know Him more deeply through this circumstantial difficulty. Dad asked, "How do you want to respond to Jesus in this?" Even at age nine, I remember my heart arising to the invitation in front of me as my emotions aligned and my focus moved out of feelings of "woe is me" into the truth of God's desire to bring me nearer in relationship to himself. I responded with a "yes" to Jesus' invitation, and the Lord answered this response by moving my little heart out of darkness and into light—just as He is always faithful to do.[10]

This week a pastor called me. His heart was torn and he was discouraged. Because he was able to pour out his heart, and was reminded to think about and find God's greater perspective, he was renewed.

To follow Jesus, everyone needs personal help

Why make disciples? If Jesus needed help, how much more do those who seek to follow Him need tangible help? Everyone I know needs someone to be Jesus to help him or her walk as Jesus walked (1 John 2:3-6).

The people in our churches need this kind of access to Jesus in the flesh. Each week, each person makes hundreds of decisions—with or without consulting Jesus—and lives are shaped and futures determined. We need routine, caring conversations that help us bring our experiences and thoughts to Jesus. Is it happening?

Jesus called His disciples to completely and fully lay down their lives for Him.[11] So He calls us, and calls us to help our disciples, to lay down our lives for Him (chap. 11). It is a call to heart and life holiness. Most of us need more than Scripture and the Holy Spirit; we need Christlike mentors.

Why do you think Jesus focused on discipling just a few people? What is the greatest reason we, as Christ-followers, should intentionally make disciples? Are there other reasons?

Most of the pride, selfishness, unforgiveness, gossip, slander, pornography, divorce, and other sins that occur among Christians are not because Christians are unaware or indifferent to them, but because there is a lack of relational mentoring in grace and truth that Jesus commanded us to provide for each other. If we would dare to obediently prioritize our time to help a few, who are then taught to help a few, who are discipled to help a few, and so on, we would be shocked at the growth of Christlikeness in our churches and the evangelism in our communities.

▶ **My Thoughts**

4 — IS MAKING DISCIPLES OPTIONAL?

Make disciples *(Matt. 28:19)*.

Making Christlike disciples is our Commander's mission

While I was a youth pastor and then a student at seminary, I studied Jesus' pattern for disciplemaking in the Gospels. A strategy for making disciples was evolving in my mind. I intensively studied the biblical record of Jesus' ministry, filling yellow pads of paper with exhaustive notes.

Then, in my first full-time pastoral responsibility, I finalized the mission and ministry. The mission: to follow, become like, and reproduce Jesus. The priority in ministry: to make disciples the way Jesus did.

Disciplemaking ministry

Debbi and I took off with great zeal. How amazing that she would regularly get up before 5 A.M. to meet with other couples who had consented to be discipled once a week starting as early as 6 A.M. Thirteen brave couples let us invade their homes each week to practice discipling on them.

Our discipling strategies were neither soft nor passive. Anyone who wanted to be discipled needed to have a serious commitment. Those being discipled had to be accountable for a daily meeting with Jesus, informal and formal discipling experiences with their families, ministry in the church, and intentional ministry with lost friends and neighbors. There were great variations in their weekly reports.

In two years, mostly through those thirteen couples, over seventy adults repented and became Christ-followers. Seven house churches were planted, growing to a weekly average attendance of about one hundred and thirty, most of whom were new to our congregation. Our worship attendance grew from about one hundred and twenty to almost two hundred. We were of one mind. Whether we were on a men's retreat, on a ski trip, or in the foyer on Sunday, normal conversations focused on Jesus, His work, and what we were experiencing in the process. He was our life. We were being disciples and making disciples of Jesus. The disciplemaking house churches and new Christians made all the study, praying, and work well worth it. We were having fun.

Heartache

Disciplemaking is not without heartache however. One night, about four and a half years into the process, I received a report of a disciple dropping out. This triggered memories of four years of intensively and personally investing in people, with several who had dropped out for various reasons. The deep disappointment was heart-wrenching and long-lasting. Focusing on the few is not without pain. Disciplemakers must be willing to invest deeply in others, with great confidence that God is delighted with our obedience and will make possible Kingdom growth through every seed we plant.

Despite the heartache, I had my mission—His mission. I had Spirit-empowered resolve to continue my mission. I even had a little vision, for I had dozens of times multiplied out what would happen if each house church pastor discipled one person to become a house church pastor, who discipled one person, and so on. I knew full well that if everyone made and multiplied one of those kinds of disciples each year, we would theoretically win the whole world in about 33 years. Did I really believe it would happen? No. Did it excite me to think about it? Yes.

(Note: Prioritizing disciplemaking does not guarantee growth in numbers. I have pastored two churches for almost ten years each, another church for almost five years, and am in the eighth year with my current congregation. Two of those churches nearly doubled in attendance. Two actually decreased in attendance.)

Tangible vision

Another mind-transforming event occurred in my life. Late one night I was reading a book written by a former Communist party leader who had become a Christian.[1] It was written neither to refute nor support Communism. It was written to reveal the strategies that enabled the Communists to grow. In just fifty years, they multiplied from a small band of seventeen men to a powerful world force that dominated one-third of the world and intimidated the other two-thirds.[2]

As I read the book, zeal and passion welled up in my mind and emotions. I would shout: "The Communists did what Jesus did!"

The concepts, applications, even words I had written down in my yellow pads were in this book. The core strategies (not values or worldview) that the Communists employed were virtually identical to those I had discovered in Jesus' disciplemaking ministry.

As I continued to read, I would occasionally lay the book down and pace, with tears streaming down my face. The Communists had changed the world in just a few decades by employing Jesus' disciplemaking strategies. And they did it without God's Word and Spirit for direction and power. My heart was broken that Jesus' Church had watered down His disciplemaking mandate and ministry.

I read on. My original vision intensified. What would happen if Jesus' people—the Church around the world—were to take seriously our Master's mandate to go into the world and make disciples? So many Christians are confused and half-hearted because they have not been discipled to authentically know and follow Jesus; no one has lived with them as Jesus lived with His disciples. What if this were different? What if Christians became leaders in the cause of Christ instead of remaining confused, half-hearted followers? What would happen if the leaders in Christ's Church would make—after prayer—the top priority of their ministry to invest in a few, who would then be equipped to focus on their few, and so on?

The vision was getting clearer. What would happen if each congregation had just one person committed not only to being a leader in Christ's cause but also to making leaders for Christ? What would happen if a ministry of disciplemaking were to spring up in every church?

The vision was now burning in my heart. One pastor could not reach the world, but all of the world could be reached if there were leaders in every church committed to multiplying other leaders.

What do you think of the idea that Jesus' disciplemaking principles are the same principles that have mobilized other massive movements? Do you think Jesus was operating with Spirit-given genius by investing in a few to reach the masses? Why or why not? What do you think about the methods churches are presently employing? How much typical programming can a church do and still have time and energy available to make disciples the way Jesus did?

I dreamed of what should and could be. I wondered how I could bring others to see the necessity of following Jesus' model of disciplemaking. I decided I could do very little, except work faithfully where I was.

I had a theoretical vision by doing the multiplication. But when I saw in real life what the Communists had done, and I saw how they did it, my vision no longer felt theoretical. I knew it could—and should—be done. I often wondered what Jesus felt as He watched us doing all kinds of things He had not told us to do while neglecting to do the things He had done and told us to do.

Dumbing down of discipleship

Interestingly, *discipleship* suddenly became the new buzzword. Sadly, for many people, making disciples got watered down to "classroom teaching and curricula." We changed the name of our Sunday School classes from Christian Education to Discipleship but basically kept things as they had been. We thought we were making disciples by merely informing people. We were teaching them, but without a discipling relationship—including accountability—we were not teaching them to obey everything Jesus taught (Matt. 28:20). Most leaders failed to take time to disciple a few people to be actual disciples of Jesus and to influence them to disciple others. The good news is that there have been and continue to be individuals, churches, and movements that are faithfully making disciples.

(Note: As Debbi and I were excitedly discipling thirteen couples, a dramatic event occurred in our lives: she gave birth to triplets. Shortly thereafter, the Holy Spirit convicted me that our family was to be our first and primary group of disciples. As the years rolled along, I came to another dramatic conclusion: the church's very best opportunities to make disciples—for many reasons—are family relationships. Until the church disciples parents to effectively and proactively disciple their children, we will miss God's highest plan and continue to lose ground in the battle for the souls of individuals and a culture.)[3]

Are *all* to be disciplemakers?

There are some men who will never become fathers and some women who will never become mothers—for very legitimate reasons. However, it is not surprising or abnormal for an adult to become a parent. In fact, it is still relatively normal.

So it is with maturing Christians regarding spiritual children. Jesus intends it to be normal—allowing for some legitimate exceptions—that mature Christians have or adopt spiritual children, that is, become disciplemakers. The tragic tale we must face is that Christlike disciplemakers in the local church are not the norm, although they should be. Almost everyone in the local church should be discipled toward becoming a Christlike disciplemaker. Some may—due to psychological or sociological disorders—never become disciplemakers, but that should be the exception, not the rule.

How do we know that making disciples is to be the norm, not the exception?

In Matt. 28:18-20, our King gives the Great Commission. In future chapters we will study the profound implications of going and baptizing and teaching to obey. Now we examine a greatly ignored command of Jesus because one word has been overlooked. The overlooked word is *everything:* "Therefore go and make disciples of all nations, baptizing them in the name of the Father and of the Son and of the Holy Spirit, and teaching them to obey *everything* I have commanded you" (vv. 19-20, emphasis added).

Everything! In the clearest language, Jesus requires that everyone who has become a Christian be taught to obey everything He commanded.

Everything includes obedience to this particular command: make disciples. Here is how it is intended to play out:

- Jesus commands me (first generation) to make disciples (second generation) who obey Jesus. As I do this, I become a spiritual parent to my disciples.
- Jesus further commands me to teach my disciples to obey everything Jesus taught, which includes making disciples. As I obediently teach my disciples to make disciples, I become a spiritual grandfather to my disciples' spiritual children (third generation). My role is not to disciple my spiritual grandchildren, but to do whatever it takes for as long as it takes to help my spiritual children do well in discipling their spiritual children.

This may sound extreme, even impossible. Not so. It is not nearly as difficult as most people believe. This book will describe, step by step, how normal Christians can be mentored to make disciples.

In 2 Tim. 2:2, Paul articulates this same multiplication of disciplemakers: "And the things you have heard me say in the

presence of many witnesses entrust to reliable men who will also be qualified to teach
others." The things Timothy (one of Jesus'
third-generation disciples) has heard from
Paul (one of Jesus' second-generation disciples), Timothy is to entrust to reliable men
(Timothy's disciples—fourth generation)
who then will be qualified to teach others
(their disciples—fifth generation). This is
the leadership multiplication Jesus modeled
and commands to reach the nations.

Are there any justifiable reasons for not intentionally making disciples?

The goal in discipling others is light-years beyond infant
Christians becoming stable and staying in the local church—as
desperately needed as that initial step is. It includes, but is well beyond, helping new Christians clean up their messes, even quit making so many messes. The goal is well beyond teaching them to feed
themselves, to walk and talk as Christ-followers. It is even beyond
helping them to serve and to be a positive influence through their
faith, faithfulness, holiness, and sacrifice. The goal is to disciple
every believer to the point of obeying all that Jesus taught, which
includes intentionally and strategically making disciples.

Vision casting

I have had conversations with many full-time secularly employed men that went something like this:

"If you are willing to

- meet with me one time per week for ten years
- meet with Jesus and your family consistently
- and simultaneously give ten years inviting every person
possible to your home to meet with you one time per week

I believe God will empower you to have a more productive

ministry than most full-time pastors have had in forty years of ministry."

Imagine with me, in language more familiar to many, what making disciples and disciplemakers could look like.

Imagine some of our senior adults who experienced the very best of what Sunday School ever was—a group of people who meet together weekly to care for each other, to seek God and His will together, and to help each other make progress in following Jesus.

To these, making disciplemakers might look like:

- A Sunday School teacher meets with his or her class in someone's home or public place.[4]
- The teacher takes all the years necessary to help everyone in the class who is willing to mature in Christ, including starting a class in each of their homes (second generation of disciplemakers).
- The Sunday School teacher (first-generation disciplemaker) lays down his or her life to help these disciples (second-generation disciplemakers) help all those in their classes start classes in their homes (third-generation disciplemakers).

Assuming 12 per class, and perfection of multiplication (which is a naive assumption, but with God all things are possible), generation 1 produces 12 disciples, generation 2 produces 144 disciples, generation 3 produces 1,728 disciples, generation 4 produces 20,746 disciples, generation 5 produces 248,832 disciples, and so on. Would this be worth 20 to 40 years of investing in 12 disciples who are discipled to invest in their 12 who invest in their 12, and on and on?

Jesus' joy

The heart of Jesus, broken when just one soul dies, tingles with excitement when He sees our renewed hearts passionately, resolutely, strategically committed to being and making Christlike disciples and mentors. He knows making Christlike disciplemakers is the best and fastest way to reach the world. As the King of kings, He commands and expects His followers to make disciples and mentors. One day He will inspect what He now expects.

We need every resource possible to strengthen our resolve to make disciples and disciplemakers. Jesus, marrying great love for His Church with compassion for deceived unbelievers, looks us straight in the eye and says, "Make disciples." Numerous pressures will call out to us to ignore Jesus and His call to make disciples. We dare not ignore Jesus or His commands:[5]

- Jesus became the source of eternal salvation for those who obey Him (Heb. 5:9).
- We know we have come to know Jesus if we obey Him and walk as He walked (1 John 2:3-6).
- Not everyone who calls Jesus Lord will enter the kingdom of heaven, but those who do the will of God (Matt. 7:21).

(Note: Worship services, the preaching of God's Word, and intercessory prayer are most helpful in being and making Christlike disciples. It is the proliferation of good but nonessential event preparation, traditions, preferences, administrative functions, and expectations that steal the precious time necessary to be and make disciples.)

Have we seen enough chaos in our families, churches, and on the news to recognize that children—both physical and spiritu-

If we prioritize being discipled and making disciples—regardless of the cost to our events and traditions—would Jesus be pleased? What would it cost? What do you think the results would be?

al—need personal, Christlike coaching to mature toward that which God intends as normal?

My motivation to make disciples is well beyond the benefits to family, church, and world. One day I will be eye to eye with Him who loves me and gave himself up for me. I desire to say to Him, "I did what You told me to do" (see John 17:4).

▶ My Thoughts

_____

_____

_____

_____

_____

_____

_____

_____

_____

_____

_____

_____

_____

_____

_____

5 — STEP ONE FOR EVERYONE

Go . . . baptizing them in the name of the Father and of the Son
and of the Holy Spirit *(Matt. 28:19-20).*

From why to how

The purpose of chapters 1—4 is to help readers recognize
and respond to God's call: to be discipled and make disciples.

Now, we move to the challenging question: How? How do I
make Christlike disciples? The question is similar to, "How do I
raise my children?" Who would dare to answer? There are countless processes and programs available for consideration. To make
disciples, we must be strategic. Strategy requires methods, from
subtle to sophisticated. All the methods of the following chapters are as biblically based as I have been able to discern and implement. Everyone must prayerfully discern God's will regarding
methods. The "how" of methods must always be rooted in the
"why" of purpose and principle.

The remaining chapters outline the disciplemaking steps Jesus identifies in Matt. 28:18-20: going, baptizing, teaching, teaching to obey, teaching to obey everything.

The first step in making Christlike disciples

- is neither new nor hard
- happens to some degree in all churches
- occurs in every arena of our lives
- requires leading no one but yourself
- is informal—uses spontaneous, Christlike acts and words
- naturally leads to formal disciplemaking—purposeful, planned, consistent meetings with Jesus

Go and make disciples

The grammar of the Great Commission does not contain four commands: go, make disciples, baptize, teach to obey. It contains only one imperative verb: *make* disciples! The three participles—"going," "baptizing," and "teaching"—all modify the main verb *make* disciples.

To be grammatically accurate, the "go" of Matt. 28:19 should read, "as you are going." The tense of "go" does not mean to go just one time. It means "as you are going." Nor is the idea to only go as a missionary to another part of the world, though it certainly includes going as (and sending) cross-cultural, professional missionaries.

It simply and clearly means this: "as you are going, make disciples." Every Christ-follower is going somewhere, every day. Wherever he or she is going, while moving through the routine of that day, he or she is to be on a mission with Jesus to make disciples. How? By demonstrating Jesus' love to everyone he or she encounters, sooner or later influencing each one to come closer to Jesus.

We go home to our families. We are on a mission there. We

go to school and we work with our neighbors. We are on a mission there as well. We go to our church family, we go to the mall, and we go to the gas station and the gym. Everywhere we go, wherever we are, we are on our mission. We are missionaries to our culture. This is where we start—realizing that our life is not purposeless nor is our primary purpose to be given to some small, temporary endeavor like being president of Microsoft. Dare you say it out loud? "I am Jesus' missionary, and wherever I am going, I intend to be on my mission of helping others move one step closer to Him."

Baptizing

But how do we help others move one step closer to Jesus?

Baptize them. Baptize? Everyone knows what that means, right? To baptize means to immerse new converts in water or pour or sprinkle water on them.

That is not exactly what I mean. The text says, "baptizing them in the name of the Father and of the Son and of the Holy Spirit," and this is indeed referring to water baptism, the public rite that initiates new believers in the community of faith; it's an outward sign of inward grace, declaring to all the new life a person has in Christ. Baptizing a person *into* (the translation of the Greek word *eis*) the name of the triune God is a way of saying that he or she is a special possession of God and is now under His authority, serving in His realm. The tense of "baptizing" also indicates that baptism is an ongoing practice in disciplemaking. Each disciple is to receive baptism.

Moreover, the word "baptize" in biblical times was used in different ways. But in each case the change from one condition to another is the common meaning. For example, when a white piece of cloth was dipped in purple dye, the intent was to effect a change from white to purple. At that point, the cloth was said to be "baptized." So baptism is about entering into something new. For each Christ-follower this is usually a one-time event.

But to get back to what I mean when I refer to baptism, I am thinking of the actual immersion that happens when something is baptized. The white cloth was immersed in the purple dye, for example. You might even think of the dye as influencing the cloth. In making disciples, we should, as the text says, baptize or initiate each new believer into the Body of Christ. But we should also "baptize" or immerse everyone we know—nonbelievers and believers—in the love of Christ. So for me baptism is not only an entrance rite but also an analogy of the way we as Christ-followers immerse or influence others in His love.

In the name of the Father, Son, and Holy Spirit

So as we are going, we are to be "baptizing"—intentionally immersing people in the love of Jesus. To enhance this idea further we need to look closer at the importance of names and naming in biblical times.

In our culture, a name is not necessarily a description. The name of a baby usually has significance to the parents based on parental preferences: "Where did you get that name?" "Oh, we saw it in a book and liked it." Sometimes names are given based on significant relationships. I am named after people who were important to my parents: Harold after my uncle, Okley after my dad, Arthur after my grandfather and another uncle. But none of those names were descriptions of me.

In ancient culture, names were much more a description of the character and activity of a person. We speak much with the names of God. His names describe His nature and His activity. Jesus is named the Lamb of God because of what He did. When character or activity changed, often a change of name would occur. Abram became Abraham.

As mentioned earlier, "baptizing in the name of the Father and the Son and the Holy Spirit" means to declare a person a special possession of God, but there is also present here the idea of totally immersing and influencing someone in the character and activity of the triune God.[1] And this idea is what I want to include in our analogy of "baptism" as a way of reaching out or influencing others. So taken together, we may say that immersing or "baptizing" people in the love of Jesus encompasses immersing them in the nature, character, and activity of God. Throughout the remainder of this book, unless noted otherwise, the wording "baptism in the name of" will refer to this analogous understanding.

So since God is merciful, whenever I am merciful to my coworker I am "baptizing" him or her in the name of God.

To "baptize" in Jesus' name means to immerse others in Jesus' nature and activity—to re-present Him, His actions, words, and attitudes. As His representatives on His mission, we are to be Christlike. This, in effect, says to everyone we meet that if he or she has seen us, he or she has seen Jesus. "What you have heard me say are not just my words, they are the words of Him who sent me on this mission to meet you at this checkout counter." Jesus was gentle. When we are gentle with others, we are "baptizing" them in the name of Jesus.

To "baptize" people wherever we go in the name of Jesus means we must be like Jesus; we must be holy as He is holy (1 Pet. 1:15-16). To do this, we ourselves must continuously be "baptized" by the Spirit of Jesus—immersed, influenced, overwhelmed so the old us no longer lives but Christ lives through us (Gal. 2:20). In other words, we must be influenced by God's Word and Spirit, just as Jesus was (chaps. 1, 2, 11).

So the first step in making disciples is not new, it is just said in a new way.

- "As you are going"—means to be Jesus' missionary wherever you are and whoever you are with.
- Baptizing them in Jesus' name or the name of the triune God still refers to the water baptism of new believers and their becoming a special possession of the One holding the name. But it is also an analogy for sensitively immersing or pouring or sprinkling the character and activity of Jesus on whoever you are with. It might be mercy or encouragement or joy or listening or visiting in prison. Over and over, time after time, day after day we are to "baptize" everyone around us in Jesus' name—in His love.

Empowerment to "baptize" others

Every authentic Christian is born of God's Spirit (John 3:5; Rom. 8:9). By virtue of the Holy Spirit's presence, every Christian is provisionally empowered to be Christlike and, wherever he or she goes, to be "baptizing" others in Jesus' name—in the love and ministries of Jesus.

> God has poured out his love into our hearts by the
> Holy Spirit, whom he has given us *(Rom. 5:5)*.

> I tell you the truth, anyone who has faith in me will
> do what I have been doing *(John 14:12)*.

> You will receive power when the Holy Spirit comes
> on you, and you will be my witnesses in Jerusalem
> *(Acts 1:8)*.

"Baptizing" our families

Our families are our best opportunity and primary responsibility for making Christlike disciples. While with our family, we are "baptizing"—influencing—for better or for worse. We can't help it. We are together—eating meals, in the car, making decisions, experiencing conflict. Our family is immersed by our Christlikeness or lack thereof. Our relationships are either Christlike or un-Christlike. Eternal or temporal values pour over each other. Jesus is either noticed or ignored in our conversations.

Growing up, it was mostly my dad who "baptized" or influenced me. He baptized me in Jesus' name, immersing me in many wonderful Christlike ways, but some of what he poured over me was not of Jesus.

His methods of baptism? He was the one person who consistently took time to simply converse with me. We went out for walks and rides and ice cream cones. I loved and liked him.

He came to me with grace and truth—at least his perceptions of truth. I believed what he said. It made sense. We dialogued about life issues—baseball, school, friends, dangers, work, money, church, even his ideas of God. He did not believe the Bible was inspired or that God was very active in our lives. He qualified as a functional deist.

He was "baptizing" me. He influenced, mentored, and discipled me to "be good" but not to believe God for much of anything. Decades later, the effects of his "baptizing" me—good and bad—still have influence.

> For better or for worse, most of us are allowing ourselves to be routinely "baptized." Who is "baptizing" you? Who are you "baptizing"? In whose name?

From our families (and televisions and computers), we are inevitably "baptized"—influenced and discipled. Sometimes this influence seems indelible. We absorb values, attitudes, ways of thinking, behaving, and relating from family members who are "baptizing" us in different ways. Therefore, we must intentionally choose to be continually baptized in Jesus' name by His Spirit, His Word, and His disciples. If we don't, the daily "baptizing" of all that is not like Jesus will disciple us poorly.

"Baptizing" our church families

The existence of our churches today is evidence that there have been Christlike disciples who persistently baptize their church in Jesus' name. These saints abide in Jesus, bear the fruit of His Spirit, and prove themselves to be Jesus' disciples (John 15:1-8; Gal. 5:22-23).

In our congregations, these saints pray unceasingly, releasing the Holy Spirit's power into the whole church. They "baptize" their churches by encouraging, smiling, delivering pies, teaching classes. For years they have sprinkled and immersed their church in Jesus' character and actions. Their influence informally disciples several people every Sunday. Those inspired then influence others, who are inspired to influence others, and Christ is lifted up through the whole church.

These Christlike saints have so raised our churches' spiritual temperature that many of us, immersed in those environments, chose Jesus. It was simply the saints being saints that discipled many of us to seek and follow Jesus. In this sense and at this level, churches make Christlike disciples.

Most of us have one or more of these saints as our heroes. They have been making Christlike disciples without a mission or a strategy. They simply loved Jesus and went around doing good (Acts 10:37-38). I love my church, for in it are those who by life and by word "baptize" me in more than ideas and expectations; they "baptize" me with the nature of Jesus. I love being with my church every Sunday to be "baptized" in Jesus' name.

The flip side is painfully true. To the degree that the values, the goals, the demonstrated priorities, the conversations, and the relationships in our congregations are not those of Jesus, to that degree our gatherings "baptize" each other in something other than Jesus' love. To that degree our churches are informally, unintentionally, but powerfully making disciples, but not of Jesus. To that degree the church is failing in her mission.

"Baptizing" our world

Imagine a wealthy company—let's say Lexus—inviting you to work for the company. Lexus offers you a very good salary. What your employer may not know is that wherever you go, you work for Jesus as His missionary, "baptizing" everyone around you.

Lexus builds the plant, cares for the maintenance, pays the utilities, and provides the equipment. Most importantly, Lexus pays hundreds of people to come and be with you, Jesus' missionary, for 40 hours every week.

Your mission: make disciples while working for Jesus at Lexus, grateful that your employer pays many to be with you 40 hours per week (Acts 4:13).

Your job description as Jesus' missionary:

- *Pray* consistently for Lexus, the employers, and employees.
- *Go* to work, diligently accomplishing well the tasks assigned to you, bringing great pleasure to your employer.
- *"Baptize"* every person in Jesus' name—*immersing* all around you with encouragement and appreciation, carefully building positive relationships with everyone possible; *sprinkling* questions into conversations, listening, understanding, valuing, responding, *pouring* help into known needs (physical, emotional, social) and pouring invitations into known interests (lunch, hunting, scrapbooking).

Normal Christians are called and capable of fulfilling this role in discipling lost persons toward Jesus. Whenever we are with lost people, they may think we are working together or eating lunch together or enjoying a concert together. They are right. But we are also fishing for people (Matt. 4:19). They think we are enjoying a burger together, not knowing that we are on a mission to "baptize" them in kindness, sensitivity, and service as we present Jesus.

Intentionally "baptizing"

Spontaneously "baptizing" everyone we meet in Jesus' love is the necessary first step. To follow Jesus in making disciples, we need to move beyond spontaneity to prayerfully selecting specific persons to "baptize."

My denominational leader (and one who influences me well) encourages all his pastors and congregations to intentionally pray and care for five specific pre-Christians. He calls them our "high five" and suggests we greet each other with a "high five," which reminds us to keep praying for and "baptizing" our specific five in Jesus' name. Great idea!

Another name for all of this is friendship evangelism. Whatever the name, every Christian is called to it and empowered by the Holy Spirit for it. Most will not keep at it without a committed band of "baptizers"—mentors—to whom to be accountable for specific, intentional, long-term sprinkling, pouring, and immersing (chap. 6).

Bill and Joan made disciples through baptizing strategically. They intentionally committed to immersing their next-door neighbors, John and Vicky, in Christlikeness.

They began by systematically praying for John and Vicky, then regularly inviting them to dinner. John and Vicky reciprocated, inviting Bill and Joan to their home. They became good friends. Over time, Bill and Joan talked naturally and openly, yet sensitively, about their past sins and failures, and how helpful it is to be following Jesus. They naturally told how Jesus was changing their lives. John and Vicky trusted Bill and Joan, including their story of how Jesus was saving their lives.

Debbi and I found Bill and Joan to be extremely coachable. We had been discipleship partners (meeting to help each other know and follow Jesus) for some time, including praying for and talking about how to introduce John and Vicky to Jesus. Through sensitive, caring relationships, it is natural to introduce the One who is most important to us. This may occur through talking about Jesus or offering a good book about Jesus or inviting someone to a house church or worship service.

One day, Bill gleefully told me that John and Vicky were coming with them to our Sunday morning worship service. The following Tuesday, several of us gathered in John and Vicky's home when they responded to Jesus' invitation to follow Him.

Spiritual conception was the prelude to spiritual birth. Jesus' grace and truth is the seed that makes conception possible. When His grace and truth are planted and contemplated, spiritual life is on the verge of being conceived. When the grace and truth are sufficiently understood to create saving faith through repentance, conception has resulted in new birth.

John and Vicky saw and heard Jesus through Bill and Joan. They experienced Jesus' grace and truth as the Word again became flesh, this time through Bill and Joan (John 1:14). Bill and Joan paid the price of a caring relationship so that grace and truth could be conceived, resulting in spiritual birth.

Laying the foundation for formal discipling

After their spiritual birth, how did Jesus disciple John and Vicky? By His Spirit and Word, to be sure. But Jesus tangibly lived, loved, and spoke through Bill and Joan. Therefore, John and Vicky were very willing to now be consistently and systematically discipled by Bill and Joan. A "baptizing" relationship—this is very important to realize—naturally paves the way for mentors to spiritually parent the baptized. Bill and Joan did this diligently for several years.

To help each other follow Jesus, both couples met weekly in discipling meetings, along with others in Bill and Joan's house church. By meeting consistently with Jesus, they dealt with every kind of spiritual issue imaginable. The result: John and Vicky matured as disciples, then disciplemakers.

Then, their formal discipling was dramatically disturbed. John and Vicky received a call from their Chief Shepherd and Discipler (1 Pet. 5:4) to become professional missionaries. They said yes and today are still saying yes. At this writing they annually take a significant number of young adults on mission trips to unreached people groups, with an average of 50 percent who respond to God's call to be professional missionaries.

How did John and Vicky mature enough to walk away from a university teaching profession to become missionaries? God called them through Bill and Joan's example of laying down their lives—not for career but for Jesus and people's eternal needs (1 Pet. 2:21).

Success is intentionally and sensitively "baptizing" all around us in the love of Jesus. The extraordinary response of John and Vicky is not the measure of success.

Like Bill and Joan, every Christian can disciple a specific few by "baptizing" them in Jesus' love. Yet few are able to do it without week-by-week accountability through caring discipleship partners.

So who is not able to "baptize" others in Jesus' name? Even lost people, for a variety of reasons, go around being good and doing good. How much more are we, filled with God's Spirit of love, able to love our families, church, and neighbors (Rom. 5:5; Matt. 22:39)? We can do this, and we must. It is the first and essential step in making disciples.

We can, but will we? Baptizing people—loving our neighbors—requires time. A major reason many have not had Christlike mentors or made disciples of Jesus is because we think we don't have time. Our culture is relationally impoverished because we value things more than persons; we won't slow down to work on relationships. We must rethink what we have created for ourselves to do—comparing it with what Jesus has called us to do—both at home and church (Isa. 50:10-11).

Explain "going" and "baptizing" and its importance in disciplemaking. What is the disciplemaker's role as described in this chapter? What are the three primary locations to "baptize"? How are you doing in informal "baptizing"? Strategic "baptizing"?

▶ **My Thoughts**

_____

_____

_____

_____

_____

6 — LEARNING FROM JESUS

Teaching them *(Matt. 28:20).*

To make Christlike disciples, we help them learn directly from Jesus

Jesus spent a lot of time with His Father. Jesus' disciples spent a lot of time with Him. To make disciples, I must help others spend a lot of time with Jesus. He welcomes all: "Come to me . . . learn from me" (Matt. 11:28-29).

Harry became a millionaire as a musician but quickly ran through his wealth. A missionary-pastor led Harry to Jesus and our church. There Harry heard that he could be Jesus' disciple. Be a disciple of Jesus? This was shocking to Harry.

He learned that being Jesus' disciple starts with spending a lot of time with Jesus. He learned that just like Peter had heard Jesus' words, he could hear Jesus' words through the Scriptures. The disciples had Jesus with them, but Harry had Jesus living in him in the person of the Holy Spirit. Jesus said this was better than being with Him himself.

> **But I tell you the truth: It is for your good that I am going away. Unless I go away, the Counselor will not come to you; but if I go, I will send him to you** *(John 16:7)*.

Because Jesus lives in His Body, the Church, Harry could physically see and hear Jesus through the Church. Harry was warned that Jesus' contemporary body is far from perfect, but whenever he was with born-again persons, he could anticipate Jesus' acts and words.

Harry believed and committed to being discipled. It became my privilege to disciple Harry to meet with Jesus so that Jesus could disciple Harry by His Word and Spirit even when I was not present.

I asked Harry if we could meet with Jesus at his house before work one morning each week. He agreed. There he could hear the words of Jesus by reading the Bible and sensing the Holy Spirit and possibly see and hear Jesus through our conversations.

During our Bible study time we would read a sentence or two and personalize it. (An explanation for this study method comes later in this chapter.) I would ask Harry what he heard Jesus saying to him through the words. Time after time, tears would stream down his cheeks as the Lord spoke words of affection, wisdom, and direction into his soul. No weird ideas, no strange interpretations of Scripture. Simply the written Word of God in an open heart. Harry's knowledge, faith, joy, and love increased exponentially—or so it seemed to me. He began getting up at 4:30 A.M. to be personally discipled by Jesus before heading off to work as a carpenter. His Bible was tattered from use.

When Jesus' words flow into our lives, good fruit is a result

(John 15:5). From being with Jesus, Harry changed so much that his influence grew. He effectively "baptized" his family, church, and work associates in Jesus' name.

It wasn't long until I asked Harry to lead some—then all—of our early morning meetings with Jesus. He learned quickly. Accordingly, I encouraged him to start a group meeting with Jesus for his family on Monday nights. He did. His two teenagers loved it and asked if they could invite their friends. Within weeks, forty people, mostly teens, were filling every corner of his home. Many of them, and several of their parents, became Christ-followers.

To make disciples, we are continuously "going and baptizing." Those who respond, like Harry, we inform—teach.

Teaching

Jesus' next step is teaching. Giving information is the area of disciplemaking in which we have done the best. Information is like an architect's drawing. It is the idea, the blueprint, the theory, the dream. It is absolutely necessary. It is the truth, which if known, believed, and obeyed, sets us free. Without accurate teaching, we are without light. However, teaching that is not accurately interpreted and translated into action is of little use. We must not be satisfied only to inform others (James 2:17).

To effectively introduce new believers into our local congregations, we help them learn about Jesus through

- worship services—praise, preaching, prayer.
- classes, including those for new Christians.
- initial relational discipling through excellent processes like Chic Shaver's *Basic Bible Studies.*[1] These establish short-term weekly relationships plus introduce important topical information and healthy accountability, creating the potential for long-term discipling.

- Encounters—an excellent conference being adopted by many disciplemaking churches.[2]

People often ask, "What curriculum should we use to make disciples?" The core manual for all Christians is the Bible. Why make any other book primary when we have God's Word and can listen directly to Him? Why not teach that the Bible is our core curriculum, and therefore train everyone to study and love it? I do this through group meetings with Jesus (see below). Other curricula can be wonderful teaching tools but should not replace the Bible as the staple of personal, family, and group study.

Teaching by listening

We are curriculum rich and relationship poor. Regardless of which curriculum we use, the essential component in disciplemaking is a personal relationship where learner-disciples can talk about both what they are learning and what they are doing with what they know.[3]

Lay seminary that listens

Since every local church is to equip the saints for the work of the ministry (Eph. 4:11-13), disciplemaking churches provide something like a lay seminary for those growing in disciplemaking. It needs to provide a systematic biblical study of major doctrines and ethical issues. Our lay seminary is called S.E.E.D.—Studies to Encourage and Equip Disciplemakers. It functions in this way:

- Each Sunday, students are given one of the thirty-three course assignments of *Leadership Multiplication* to study.[4]
- The following Sunday night, students gather and are given an opportunity to ask questions about the assignment.
- Next, the class is divided into groups of three (different groups each week), with one student assigned to ask questions of a second student to find out what the second stu-

dent can articulate from the study. The question asker is not allowed to teach, only to ask. The third student observes and then gives feedback both to the question asker (who is learning to lead by asking) and the student. We have learned that persons who can spot theological problems when listening often need a lot of help when it comes to articulating their perceptions. Through studying and articulating, leaders are being developed and so are meaningful relationships centered in Jesus.

We will always need one-way communication—preaching, teaching, books, DVDs, and so on. But we grossly fail Jesus and others when we fail to establish two-way communication. As a disciplemaker, the issue is much more than just what I know; it is what my disciple knows. It is more than what I do; it is what my disciple does. The only way for me to know what my disciple knows, and does, is to teach less and listen more.

We can teach one hundred or one thousand or ten thousand at once. We can only listen to one at a time. This is one reason Jesus selected only twelve to be with Him. Good disciplemakers like Jesus know their sheep (John 10:14, 27). To know our sheep, we must learn to listen. Good disciplemakers are excellent listeners. We need far more listening structures than we need teaching structures precisely because we can teach masses all at once, but we do not know what disciples are learning or doing until we ask and listen.

The issue is not what we teach but what disciples hear. What—and how much—they hear is extraordinarily unique to each person because of his or her unique heart condition: values, mind-sets, definitions, present pressures, and so on. Each one's actions will be shaped by the condition of his or her heart, including a bit of the teacher's influence. Disciplemakers teach by listening to their disciples!

Discipled by Jesus

My most important teaching task as a disciplemaker is to somehow connect my disciple with Jesus. Jesus is the Teacher and Disciplemaker; I am simply a bridge who seeks to connect a fellow disciple with our common Discipler. To help my disciples be Jesus' disciples, we meet with Jesus together. This is where I seek to create genuine communication between Jesus and my disciples.

This leads to a critical disciplemaking structure: meeting with Jesus.

Very early in my career in disciplemaking, I realized that for me to make disciples of Jesus I had to connect them with Him. How could that happen?

One day I was thinking about Peter, James, and John. They were with Jesus to watch and hear Him (Mark 3:14). I realized that I could, in fact, be discipled by Jesus too. I have Jesus' words—the Scriptures—and thus I can listen to Jesus any time I am willing. I can mentally watch Him and actually read His words like a love letter—which they are. I can learn from Him as surely as Peter, James, and John learned.

I realized that I have His Spirit available to be with me and teach me, if I will pay attention.

> But the Counselor, the Holy Spirit, whom the
> Father will send in my name, will teach you
> all things and will remind you of everything
> I have said to you *(John 14:26).*

> When the Counselor comes, whom I will send to
> you from the Father, the Spirit of truth who goes
> out from the Father, he will testify about me
> *(15:26).*

Jesus himself said having His Spirit was better than being with Him physically (16:7).

I also came to realize I could meet with Jesus because He lives through His collective body, the Church. First I needed to carefully discern which Christians' perspective and behaviors were Christlike (1 Thess. 5:21). But to become what Jesus intended me to become, I clearly needed a Christlike church to disciple me. Through Jesus' contemporary body I could actually encounter Him.

The most exhilarating component of my discovery was that Jesus has invited me to come to Him to be His disciple (Matt. 11:28-29). This was, and is, the delight of my life—to be alone with Jesus, watching, listening, and responding to Him. I can be with Him whenever I want, and He delights in being with me!

To be Jesus' disciple, I had to spend consistent time meeting with Him. This meeting became the first priority of my life. I resolved to meet with Jesus before any other activities of any day.

How to be discipled by Jesus

What follows are some key components of meeting with Jesus in order to be discipled by Him.[5] This is what Harry was discipled to do and to help others to do.

Look at Jesus

- *"Jesus, what are You like?"*

I use Scripture to learn of Jesus, recording what I learn about Him and His Father. I meditate on the implications of what I know. Using an alphabetical list of the names of God is a good way to begin. Examples:

- Author of Eternal Salvation (Heb. 5:9)
- Bread of Life (John 6:35)
- Creator (Rom. 1:25)
- Deliverer (11:26)

- Immanuel (Matt. 1:23)
- Faithful (Rev. 19:11)

Then I praise Jesus. I imagine King Jesus sitting with me. I look into His eyes, telling Him my thoughts, feelings, and commitments. This is praise and worship.

- *"Jesus, how did we do?"*

"Every good and perfect gift is from above" (James 1:17). I reflect on what has happened in my life since last meeting with Jesus. I evaluate my relationships, looking for good things, especially Christlikeness with family and others. I observe blessings that I have received from others and temporal blessings like food, eyesight, job, and so on. For so many good things, and every bit of progress, I look into Jesus' eyes and thoughtfully thank Him. He is working in me (Phil. 1:6).

Importantly, I also thank my Sovereign King for errors (mine and others) and hard things (Eph. 5:20). He could have fixed everything. Instead, for good reasons, He chose otherwise, knowing I could mature in humility, faith, love, and so on, through these challenges.

- *"Jesus, would You show me more about You?"*

I love systematically and slowly reading through the Gospels. I ask the Holy Spirit to help me know what Jesus was thinking, feeling, desiring, even why Jesus did what He did or said (Jer. 9:23-24) making sure to be careful and humble about my conclusions. Taking only one event or paragraph per meeting, I record and meditate on truth that I discover about Jesus, and tell Him my thoughts about Him. This is "spirit and truth worship" (John 4:24).

Listen to Jesus

- *"Jesus, what are You saying to me?"*

All Scripture is Jesus' written Word to us (2 Tim. 3:16). In my studies I read through one book of the Bible. Starting at the beginning, I study one paragraph—even one sentence—at a time in the following fashion:

Analyze. I am listening to the very words of Jesus and take them seriously. If I do not know the meaning of each word, I look it up in a dictionary. When I don't understand a sentence or paragraph, I consult a study Bible or commentary, or call a respected friend (Acts 8:30).

Categorize. I reread the paragraph or sentence. As I read, I look for the following categories and record one of the following symbols in the margin wherever it fits. For example, if what I read is a command, I put a *C* next to the verse.

N—for nature of God the Father, Son, Spirit

A—for activity of God the Father, Son, Spirit

P—for promise to believe

C—for commandment to obey

EX—for example to follow

W—for warning to heed

E—for error to avoid

F—for fact of not presently recognized significance

Q—for question to get help with

Personalize. Now comes the conversation. I imagine Jesus sitting with me or me sitting at His feet (Luke 10:39). He whispers to me through this Bible study by His Spirit. Without changing the meaning in the slightest—it may no longer be Jesus' Word if I do—I record in my journal Jesus saying the very words of Scripture, but in first person language from Him to me. For example, Prov. 3:5-6:

"Hal, I want you to trust Me with all your heart. I don't want you to lean on your own perspective. It is important that in all your ways you acknowledge Me. As you do this, know I am with you and will direct your path."

I am very careful to not add or detract from the precise meaning of God's Word (Rev. 22:18-19). I test any interpretations with Scripture and/or trusted friends (Acts 17:11; 1 Cor. 14:32).

- *"Lord Jesus, is there anything You want me to do in response to Your Word?"*

I am confident that there are many times I have experienced Jesus' ideas, emotions, and desires from listening to Him talk to me in this way. Sometimes I write back to Him. Sometimes I know there is something He wants (or has even told) me to do. This is very meaningful, listening to the Eternal God whisper something important to me, one of His disciples (John 15:15; 1 Cor. 2:9-10).

I repeat this process as much as possible in order to be discipled by Jesus and to become Christlike through receiving the mind of Christ (Rom. 12:2; 1 Cor. 2:16; note Phil. 3:19).

Love others with Jesus

- *"Lord, what do You want to do today?"*

The first step of partnering with Jesus in serving is intercession. In this very moment, Jesus is serving by interceding (Heb. 7:25). Having come to Him and learned of Him (Matt. 11:28-29), He calls me to unite with Him in His purposes. Since He is always interceding, He invites me to serve with Him: "Your kingdom come, your will be done, on earth as it is in heaven" (6:10).

Now I put down my pen and imagine the people and responsibilities I will encounter today. "Jesus, what do You want to do while I am with Kevin?" I trust the Holy Spirit to work through all I have learned of Jesus and to help me know what He actually wants. I ask Jesus to specifically do what I believe He wants to do, believing that He will act according to His will (John 14:13-14).

- *"Lord, what do You want to do through me today?"*

Next, I ask Jesus another question: "How do You want me to partner with You in answering this prayer?" If I discern something to do, I will be serving with Jesus.

I give the Holy Spirit time to guide me. He may show me specific ways to relate to Kevin or some other act of kindness He would like to do through me, or He may show me nothing. The key is that I give Jesus a chance to send me into ministry with His directions just as He sent His first disciples (Matt. 10; Luke 9).

I pray for Jesus' empowerment to do what I feel He is leading me to do. When I receive no direction, I ask Him to empower me to be Christlike with every person and to empower me for every task He has called me to for this day.

When I journal this meeting with Jesus, systematically recording my conversations with Him, I experience far more benefit.

I encourage everyone to give as many hours to being with Jesus as possible. You will both be glad you did. Compare the eternal benefit of being with Jesus versus going to the movies or surfing the net.

Making disciples and disciplemakers

Meeting with Jesus can be an authentic, reproducible disciplemaking process.

1. *I can be Jesus' disciple by meeting with Him.* This meeting with Jesus has disciplemaking principles built into it.
2. *I can help others be Jesus' disciples by helping them meet with Him.* Just as Jesus disciples me in our meetings, He will disciple others. I simply need to help others connect with Jesus as I do. In so doing, I am helping them be discipled by Jesus.
3. *I can train these people to be personally discipled by Jesus*

without me. Further, by repeatedly meeting with Jesus to-gether, I not only help disciple others but also train them to meet with Jesus alone. Thus, by being with Jesus, they can be personally discipled by Him.

As a fourth grader, our daughter Deborah did these three steps during her lunch hour.

4. *I can coach these people to make disciples by helping them to help their family and friends meet with Jesus.* If I can help those I am discipling truly learn the principles and processes of being discipled

> What is the disciplemaker's role in this chapter? The disciple's role?

through meeting with Jesus, then they can invite their family, their church family, and their friends to join them in meeting with Jesus. In this way not only are they being discipled personally by Jesus, but also they would be making disciples of Jesus by helping all who would meet with them to meet with Jesus.

5. *Finally, I can help these I am discipling help their disciples (family and friends) to make disciples.* Result: Christlike disciplemaking would be multiplying.

By understanding and applying these five concepts, almost anyone who is willing can greatly impact eternity by making disciples and disciplemakers. Relationships that develop around the group meeting with Jesus are normally the basis for profound coaching in obedience to Jesus, one-on-one or in the group.

Jesus spent a lot of time being discipled by His Father. Few of us will approximate Christlikeness apart from extensive rela-tionship and communication with Jesus. Further, if I am to make Christlike disciples, I will have to disciple them to spend a lot of time in direct communication with their Heavenly Father.

▶ **My Thoughts**

7 — OBEYING FROM THE HEART

Teaching them to obey *(Matt. 28:20)*.

To make Christlike disciples, we help disciples understand heart obedience

To teach our disciples is one thing; to teach them to obey is an altogether different issue. Contrary to a lot of cultural theology, the Bible is clear that obedience, with the help of the Holy Spirit, is an essential feature of authentic Christianity. To set the stage for discussing biblical obedience, consider Jim's story.

Jim had lived a horrendous life of sin. His routine battles included drunkenness, brawling, anger, abuse, and hatred. He was struggling in his fifth marriage.

A long-term friend invited him to our services. Jim sheepishly came. He looked big and tough, but he cowered under his guilt and shame. He had a hard time looking me in the eye, calling me a "man of the cloth."

Jim agreed to attend our men's retreat. Late the first night, about eight of our men jammed into a room, talking about Jesus. Nervously he sat on the fringe. At some point he expressed that he had been so bad that nothing could get him right with God. Almost everyone—one way or another—pounced on his statement, trying to explain the meaning of the Cross. He wouldn't budge.

In spite of our antics, somehow the Holy Spirit convinced Jim that his performance, regardless of how bad or how good, was not the issue. It was Jesus' perfect performance, His sacrificial death for the worst of sinners, and our confidence in who Jesus is and what He had done that frees us from condemnation and actually covers us with His righteousness. Jim had been so long bound in guilt and condemnation that it required a miracle of revelation to destroy the lies in his mind. The miracle happened, and Jim became a Christ-follower.

Struggling with sin

But what a struggle we had. Time after time, I would hear that Jim had given up. We would talk. It was always the same process: sin, discouragement, giving up on Jesus, unable to believe Jesus would not give up on him. The sin pattern was normally conflict, anger, abuse, alcohol, guilt, shame, despair.

Jim was persuaded that he was too bad to ever be a Christian. I could have agreed, which of course would have been a lie. Or I could have told him not to be so concerned about his sinfulness, because Jesus' death covered the penalty and Jim had the gift of righteousness through simple faith. The last part was true, but the part suggesting God's indifference to his sinfulness would have been terribly untrue. God is intensely concerned about sinfulness.

In our conversations, Jim could not talk about Jesus, the Cross, or forgiveness. He was too overwhelmed with his sinfulness. So time after time I would ask, "Jim, when Jesus looks at your intention, what does He see?" The answer took time, but we got his true intentions into the open.

Both discouragement and predisposition to quit were disguised demonstrations that Jim sincerely wanted and intended to obey Jesus. His heart was not indifferent to Jesus. He consistently contemplated quitting because he did not want to be a hypocrite. But underneath and mixed into his frustration was sincere intent, even desire, to quit sinning and follow Jesus. I could see that. He could not. He was naive to believe that after years of ungodly thoughts and actions he could quickly change. But he wanted to. When he finally recognized his intent to obey well enough to articulate it, I said it was perfect. He furrowed his brow, and I told him, "God sees your heart to obey and calls it perfect."

After venting about the pain regarding his sin, Jim could talk about Jesus, the Cross, and grace. He repeatedly chose to refocus on Jesus, starting with His sacrificial death for sinners that included even him so that he could be fully forgiven and accepted into God's family.

It took many conversations, but finally Jim could tell himself the truth: his relationship with Jesus was not dependent on his own righteousness or lack of it, but Christ's, and though God hated his sins, God truly evaluated Jim's authentic intent and real desire to obey and called it perfect.

Jim stabilized. He had just retired and gave many hours cleaning and fixing things at our church. One day he had a massive heart attack. One of the greatest services of my life was not long before he died. It was his baptismal service. Family and a few friends gathered around his bed and sang songs of amazing grace. We watched his eyes glisten with profound joy. His words of faith in Christ alone were clear and convincing. I poured a little water over his head. Everyone either shouted or laughed or wept—all with joy—for this saint, saved by grace through authentic faith.

Jim's story raises several issues that disciplemakers, commanded to teach their disciples to obey Jesus, need to understand.

God sees the heart

To teach their disciples to obey, disciplemakers must first, with great emphasis, teach their disciples that God clearly observes a person's heart.

> Man looks at the outward appearance, but the
> LORD looks at the heart *(1 Sam. 16:7)*.

> You are the ones who justify yourselves in the eyes
> of men, but God knows your hearts *(Luke 16:15)*.

> God, who knows the heart, showed that he
> accepted them *(Acts 15:8)*.

> And he who searches our hearts *(Rom. 8:27)*.

> Then all the churches will know that I am he who
> searches hearts and minds *(Rev. 2:23; see also John
> 7:24; Acts 1:24; 1 Chron. 28:9; 2 Chron. 16:9)*.

Our behavior is the direct by-product of our hearts. God clearly judges our behavior, but it is judgment based on the condition of the heart that caused the behavior—both good and bad. From the time of our new birth, God is at work in our hearts, increasing our love for Him and our desire to obey Him. Changes in our thinking and behavior occur as the Holy Spirit remakes us from the inside out. What is important is that our hearts are willing to be changed and are responsive to the Spirit's guidance.

Disciplemakers must help their disciples understand the difference between a willing, obedient heart and perfect performance. Failure to make this distinction has left many sincere followers of Jesus discouraged, ashamed, and so guilt-ridden they quit trying. The Holy Spirit's work takes time, and each disciple is different. All disciples benefit from the support and encouragement of a mentor and other believers. Some disciples need more attention than others. In spite of God's faithfulness, I think Jim would have quit without persistent, personal discipling.

In this chapter on obedience, why is it of ultimate importance to understand that God truly understands and evaluates us first by our heart's condition?

Some people who cannot distinguish between performance and having a right heart do not quit, but rather adopt a culturally demonstrated set of Christian "requirements," which are quite easy to accomplish. Keeping these "requirements" as justification for a relationship with God is legalism, as is quitting for not being good enough.

Others who cannot distinguish between performance and having a right heart go to the other extreme by theologically rationalizing disobedience to God, "trusting God" for their salvation while willfully tolerating known sin or blatantly ignoring God's clear commandments. This is cheap grace. To teach disciples to obey, disciplemakers must help their disciples avoid these errors.

The key: teach your disciples that God requires obedience, but it is relational heart obedience—the responsive commitment to God's Self-revelation. As your disciples get to know God better, and as His Spirit works in their lives, their love for Him will increase and so will their desire and ability to obey Him.

God requires an obedient heart

Having established that God judges us by our hearts, the disciplemaker's next task is to help disciples establish a heart to obey. By this I mean authentic *resolve* to obey Jesus. If they have not established this resolve earlier, the water baptism of converts is a good time for them to establish and articulate their determination to obey Jesus. It is a vow, the position of the heart. Though our performance will be imperfect, the vow to seek, believe, and obey can and must be sustained as the intent of the heart.

Jesus' death can free us from the slightest fear of rejection due to our imperfect performance. Grace frees us to "aim for perfection" (2 Cor. 13:11) without fear of failure. The aiming is what delights God. Those who fearlessly aim inevitably improve in hitting the mark. That's part of the Holy Spirit's work in their lives.

We must teach our disciples to resolutely set their will, with the Holy Spirit's help, to obey Jesus. Why?

The first reason: the Bible emphatically requires obedience as necessary to salvation.

Note some New Testament statements about obedience:

> Not everyone who says to me, "Lord, Lord," will
> enter the kingdom of heaven, but only he who does
> the will of my Father who is in heaven *(Matt. 7:21).*

> The Lord Jesus . . . will punish those who do not
> know God and do not obey the gospel of our

Lord Jesus. They will be punished with everlasting
destruction and shut out from the presence
of the Lord and from the majesty of
his power *(2 Thess. 1:7-9).*

Although he was a son, he learned obedience from
what he suffered and, once made perfect, he
became the source of eternal salvation for all
who obey him *(Heb. 5:8-9).*

We know that we have come to know him if we
obey his commands. The man who says, "I know
him," but does not do what he commands is a liar,
and the truth is not in him. But if anyone obeys his
word, God's love is truly made complete in him.
This is how we know we are in him: Whoever
claims to live in him must walk as Jesus did
(1 John 2:3-6).

A dangerous misinterpretation of these scriptures can make
it seem like perfect behavior is required to be saved. If we believe
this to be absolute, flawless perfection, we find ourselves in the
hopeless search for righteousness through works.

This is precisely why I interpret these scriptures on obedience
from the perspective that God sees and evaluates us by our hearts.
Speak emphatically about obedient hearts. Disciples must understand that when God talks about obedience, and looks for it, He
is talking about our hearts. As the Holy Spirit remakes our
hearts, these scriptures become a reality in what we think and do.

So an obedient heart toward God is primarily about relationship with God. Relationship is precisely why He made us. It is
most reasonable to assume that what God cares about in our

obedience is first of all our relationship with Him, which is revealed by the condition of our heart.

I have an obedient heart when I'm determined to obey God. I may not know what to obey, but the Holy Spirit will guide me and help me. When my will is set to obey, I have an obedient heart. Jesus' words of encouragement to His fumbling, sleeping disciples were, "The spirit is willing, but the body is weak" (Matt. 26:41).

God knows precisely when we intend to obey Him, but due to ignorance and/or weakness, we fall. If we *intend* to obey, we will either obey or face our struggle and seek help. Perfect!

God also knows precisely if we are indifferent or unwilling to obey His commands. Indifference and unwillingness—both functions of the heart—reveal absence of faith in Him or clear rebellion, and regardless of how good we may look on the outside, He sees and judges us by our unwilling hearts. This is a desperate condition for anyone to be in before God.

> Do you agree or disagree that God requires obedience to be in His family? Why or why not? Why does heart obedience strike a balance between cheap grace and legalism?

A thoughtful study of the many texts that teach God's judgment based on our hearts is paramount. It is equally paramount that disciples be taught to carefully guard their heart, because the complex components of the heart—information storage, attitudes, memories, emotions, desires, motives, and so on—influence the will (Prov. 4:23).

Even with obedient hearts, there is much more that lies

ahead. We will still grow and mature with ever-increasing acts of obedience as the Holy Spirit works in us.

Teach your disciples these three facts:

1. God cares first about the heart.

2. God requires obedience.

3. It is heart obedience that God requires.

Then teach them clearly what heart obedience is.

Teaching disciples how to respond to un-Christlikeness

Every disciple needs to be able to explain to his or her mentor what he or she does when dealing with un-Christlikeness. Following are some important steps a disciple must go through when he or she has been un-Christlike:

- Confess
  - Ungodliness (1 John 1:9)
  - Faith (Rom. 10:9; Phil. 2:11)
- Celebrate
  - The Holy Spirit has not left you: "Thank You for showing me. This reveals that You have not left me and deeply love me" (see John 16:8-13).
  - Being a new creation (2 Cor. 5:17). The pain you feel when you come short of God's will is a sign of being new. Before becoming a follower of Jesus, little or no pain existed for missing God's will.
  - Being a child of God—not based on your own godliness, but on Christ's (Titus 3:3-7).
- Correct (Rom. 12:21)
  - Go to anyone hurt by ungodliness (Matt. 6:23-24; Acts 19:18).
  - Ask and believe God for help in growing (1 John 1:9).
  - Dialogue with mentor about what influenced this un-

godly behavior and what can be done to overcome evil with good.

Our disciples' times of error are usually the best teaching times. Use them well (James 1:2-8; 5:16). For example, when a disciple shares about his or her fears, mentors might respond something like this:

> *When we have made errors in following Jesus, why does running to Jesus resolve the problem? What should happen?*

- Thank you for sharing this fear. Do you understand the cause of your fear? What do you think about being afraid for those reasons? As you think about these fears, where is the Lord in your thinking? Can you imagine what He thinks about your fears? What has He said? Are you able to believe Him?
- Now that we see and have confessed your fear, is there anything to celebrate and learn?
- What needs to be corrected? With whom? How?

Three responses to grace every disciple must be able to explain to his or her discipler

Saving faith. If I have faith in my doctor, I will do what he or she says. If I do not want to know what he or she thinks and do what he or she says, I clearly do not have faith in him or her. The same is true about faith in Jesus (John 1:12; 3:16, 36; 5:24; 6:47; 8:24; Acts 16:31; Rom. 3:24-26; 5:1; Gal. 2:20; Eph. 2:8; James 2:17; 1 John 5:10-12).

Repentance is much more than feeling sorrow for my sin (2 Cor. 7:8-11). It is a genuine change of mind from self-reliance and self-government to relying on Jesus and seeking His government (Rom. 2:5; 2 Pet. 3:9; Luke 13:1-5; 24:46-47; Acts 2:38; 3:19; 5:31; 8:22; 11:18; 20:21; Matt. 3:8).

Why do both authentic faith and repentance inevitably result in determination to obey Jesus? How does a discipler help a discouraged disciple who is struggling with sin? A disciple apparently not too concerned about sin? What is the discipler's responsibility from this chapter? The disciple's?

Heart obedience is authentic resolve to obey God from a heart of love. It inevitably leads to increased Christlikeness or to getting help in challenging areas (see references above and note also Matt. 5:17; 6:24; 19:17; Luke 6:46-49; 8:21; 12:47-48; 14:26-35; John 10:27; Acts 4:19; 5:29; 6:7; Rom. 1:5; 2:7-8; 6:15-18; 8:4-5; 15:18; 16:26; 2 Cor. 5:15; Eph. 5:6; Titus 1:16; 3:3-7; Heb. 11:8-10; James 2:14-26; 1 John 2:17; 3:24; 2 John 9; Rev. 12:11; 17:14).

▶ **My Thoughts**

_____

_____

_____

_____

_____

_____

_____

_____

_____

8 — THINKING WITH JESUS

We take captive every thought to make it obedient to Christ *(2 Cor. 10:5)*.

To make Christlike, obedient disciples, we help them think with Jesus about their hearts

The purpose of chapters 8 and 9 is to help our disciples *think* about their hearts and Jesus' heart, on their own, throughout each day. Why? Conscious dialogue with Jesus empowers obedience to Him.

The processes of chapters 8 and 9 are the most important of this book because they are necessary for most people and are the least practiced part of disciplemaking models, families, and churches.

The processes? Dialogue with a disciple about his or her story, heart, and the truth so that person learns to come to heart-truth individually. In practice this is having *intentional* conversations where a mentor *listens* to a disciple tell his or her story, discover his or her heart, and think with Jesus about his or her story and heart.

There is a time to teach. Then comes the time to ask about our disciples' perspectives. There is a time to call to action. Then comes the time to listen to the actions and hearts of our disciples.

Christlike disciplemakers know—are intimately acquainted with—their disciples (John 10:14, 27). For this to occur, disciplemakers must intentionally listen to and understand their disciples, especially their walk with Jesus. To listen more, we must talk less (James 1:19). To listen better, we learn to ask better questions.

While studying how Jesus made disciples, I noticed that He asked many questions. And He was with His disciples most of the time. We must ask questions of our disciples to have them tell us their stories, for we cannot be with them most of the time. Asking disciples effective questions helps both disciple and disciplemaker discover the heart and then learn Jesus' perspective.

With our disciples we must figure out how to build the relationships and establish the structures where their lives are the curriculum for study and support. My best disciplemaking experiences have been a combination of the formal meetings (chaps. 6 and 11) and regularly scheduled meetings having no agenda except to discover a person's story and heart and Jesus' perspective.

Through this process, there is progress.

To illustrate, look at the following situation from my older son's life. The conversations demonstrate the necessity of disciplemakers listening, asking questions, and working with their disciples' stories, hearts, and truth.

A story about life, heart, and truth

One of our triplets, David, quit growing in the second grade. His existing relationships minimized negative ramifications, but as he entered seventh grade, we moved to Oklahoma City. He left a small Christian school where he had been a popular leader and entered a 1,600-member junior high school, standing one to two feet shorter than all his peers and looking several years younger.

I began to notice a change in David just a few days into his seventh grade adventure. I noticed that for several days in a row he had not met me at the door as usual. Instead, I had to go looking for him.

"Hey, Bud?" I called out to him. Silence. I ran up the stairs to his room and knocked.

"Hey, Pal, are you in there?"

"Yeah," he answered in a quiet, slightly distressed tone.

"May I come in?"

"OK."

I entered to find him crumpled up on his bed. This was uncharacteristic of my outgoing junior high son. He stood up as I came in. The pain in his face told me he was not OK. I knelt on one knee, wanting to look into his eyes. But his eyes were riveted on anything but mine.

"What's up, Pal?"

"Nothin'."

"C'mon. You can tell me."

Silence.

"Did they jam you in a locker again? Steal your clothes? What happened?" I am searching for his story. It had become increasingly difficult this September.

"What did they call you today?" Silence.

David and I had been meeting privately every week for years. We had many discussions where both of us shared deeply of our thoughts, emotions, and desires. But in one short month, it was rapidly changing. His new junior high career had been shocking and painful.

"Hey, kid," other students would taunt, "the kindergarten is down the street." "Who let you in here? Go back to grade school!" Relentless mocking and rejection were just the beginning. In gym class his classmates thought it great fun to hide, even destroy, the "little kid's" underclothes. They would see if they could stash him in a locker. One boy on the football team, whom I'll call "Ryan," was nearly twice David's weight. He took great delight in consistently punching David, just for fun.

Although the damage to David's body was minimal, the damage to his heart was enormous. Right before our eyes, our happy, confident, fun, friendly son was becoming a sullen, angry, hostile loner. His behavior changed drastically and immediately. To be sure, the abuse was the catalyst of these changes, but the core problem and cause was in his heart.

Heart damage

By heart, I mean the personality. The heart includes:
- thoughts, ideas, memories, attitudes[1]
- emotions—fear, peace, sadness, joy, anger, hostility, guilt, rejection, shame, futility[2]
- desires to be loved, safe, secure, valuable, significant, fulfilled[3]
- motives of every kind[4]
- will—the capacity to choose direction, to oppose internal or external pressures[5]

Try to imagine the damage to David's heart when his peers verbally and physically abused him. How would your *thoughts* change if you went from being one of the most popular, cool kids on campus to being mocked and beaten daily? You might have different thoughts about yourself, the future, school, your peers, your parents, and even about the God whom you had come to believe was your Protector. You might respond with the *emotions* of fear, insecurity, resentment, anger, hostility, hatred, or guilt.

What about your *desires*? You might never want to go back to school. Or you might want revenge. Or you might want to find someone, anyone, to make you feel better. What about your *motives*? Would you be able to dig down to the core reasons for the way you feel or for the way you are acting at home? Would you be able to unpack the confusion in your heart and sort out the core reasons why you are now filled with fear, anger, and hate? You might come to new *conclusions* about God, yourself, and your tormentors. Would your conclusions be accurate? Consider how your conclusions would affect every other area of your life now and a decade or so later. As a man "thinks in his heart, so is he" (Prov. 23:7, NKJV).

Would you be able to guard your heart from godless and immature reactions?

We, and our disciples, have heart damage like David did. We can't go through life without being wounded. These wounds, if not cared for, will damage or disable us. Do our disciples know how to care for the wounds in their hearts? Rarely.

It was to this son with a severely wounded heart that I asked my questions about surviving the day at school. Our disciples go through painful mental-emotional battles. Will they tell us about them?

Ask caring questions

"If you are willing, I'd love to hear about your day."

Depending on the day, I would hear different scenarios. Sometimes kids pulled his hair; other times it was the locker routine. Sometimes it was just being pushed or sworn at or verbally mocked. We counted up to fifteen offenses one day. I listened to his story and then responded by asking a heart-opening question like, "Can I ask how that made you feel?"

Note the question. I was knocking at the door of his personal, secret emotions. At first, his response was guarded, but when he realized that I really wanted to know his true feelings without judgment, it was OK to open his heart. Out came statements like, "I'm afraid. Mad. I can't stand them." My response was, "I don't blame you."

As is essential in every component of disciplemaking, our disciples must know that our motive is to genuinely help them.

Empathy opens and connects hearts

Simple empathy is a good way to come up with questions. Try to imagine what you might be thinking or feeling or desiring if you were in this person's situation. If the question probes too deeply or feels too difficult, you're knocking too hard. Be gentle and humble, like Jesus (Matt. 11:29).

I empathetically asked David questions based on what I think I would have felt if it were happening to me. "Do you wish you could get even? Do you wish someone would punch them for you?"

To unpack a heart, knock gently at the door by asking questions about a thought or an emotion or a desire. For David, "Do you wish you could get even?" was a question that knocked on the door of desire.

If you have a strong, positive relationship, you will better know what to ask and what not to ask. Be sure not to assume your disciple feels what you might feel. Guard against your disciple feeling pressure from you to say something he or she really does not think or feel. Anything other than absolute truth will only confuse the issues. We are after truth in the innermost parts because the truth sets us free (John 8:32).

Thank you for opening your heart

Sometimes, after David shared his feelings with me, I would

say something like, "I am so sorry. I know I can't feel what you feel. Thank you for telling me some of it." His response was often silence. Mine was often to hug him again. Though I felt angry and frustrated at what was happening to him, I believe the Holy Spirit gave me ways to work the most important truths deeply into Dave's heart through careful questions.

When your disciple shares something from the heart, be extremely sensitive with your response. This person's heart is a secret, private, personal treasure. Your tone, if not your very words, should say, "Thank you for the gift of trusting to me your hidden feelings."

When someone shares his or her heart, it seems almost impossible not to pour out your heart in return. We want to teach, argue, blame, defend, correct, disagree, judge. But guard your heart. Let your will govern your thoughts and emotions. Try to respond empathetically: "I'm so sad to hear that . . ." "That must have really hurt . . ."

Your disciple's heart-components are either Christlike or not. Because we are governed by our heart-components, we need to get them out in the open to see and consider what to do with them.

Opening my heart: expressing love appropriately

When appropriate, expressing our genuine valuing of our disciples greatly helps.

"David, Pal, what do I think about you?" Silence. "I'm serious, Pal. Are you important to me?"

"Yes." The weak, subdued answer finally came.

My son and I had talked about thoughts and emotions for years, particularly about love between family members, friends, and Jesus. To raise the issue of my personal valuing of David was my attempt to help him think about his situation from a greater perspective than he was capable of on his own. I wanted to get a *truth* that makes a difference firmly planted in my son's mind, either by replacing a lie or establishing truth of greater significance than a secondary fact.

"If you really believe that you are important to me, does that make any difference in how you think or feel about what the kids at school think about you?" By now, we are actually able to have a fairly reasonable conversation about a very difficult topic. I waited for his answer, which usually did not come. Then I would answer my own question. "Probably not much difference. But think with me."

Planting Jesus' love and will into the heart

I asked the following questions very deliberately, when I was confident that David was ready to consider each question.

"Do you really believe Jesus is real and alive?" I asked.

"Yes," David answered.

"Are you sure?"

"Yes."

I kept on.

"Is He always with you?"

"Yes."

"Does He know everything that is happening to you at school?"

"Yes."

"Does He have all power to stop what is happening or to change it?"

"Yes."

"If He loves and values you, is that a big deal?"

"Yes."

"Do you know that Jesus really loves you?

"Yes."

"Are you important to Him?"

> **What will happen to Christians if they seldom talk about Jesus or their struggles in responding to life's challenges His way? What benefits occur from consistent talks about responding to life's challenges His way?**

"Yes."

Sometimes yes-no questions are valuable instead of open-ended questions. After each question I would wait for David to think and respond. Notice that each question was aimed at a most foundational, basic, theological truth that almost every new Christian is able to affirm. I simply wanted David to think about and affirm Truth greater than the mess he experienced at school. Our disciples routinely need to have big, eternal truth brought next to the small, temporal facts that are governing their minds, emotions, desires, and wills.

By that time in the process, David's answers were coming more quickly and with increasing certainty. I watched with my own eyes. Time after time, when somehow we got to the bottom line of Jesus' presence and love, I watched the power of the Holy Spirit working in a devastated seventh grader's mind. God's truth planted in the mind is normally the key to heart health.

From a devastated heart to a discipled heart

About this time, the truth started to set David free. His head would lift, we might lock eyes for the first time in the conversation, and he would answer, "Yeah . . . yeah!"

The facts that he was small and that kids at school were making life miserable for him were gradually being overshadowed by a major truth. The major but difficult truth was and is that the King of the universe is on his side. David is infinitely valuable to Jesus. This great King is always with him, loving him, and able to stop the storm or give David something better: the ability to overcome evil with good and reveal the very character of Jesus. The greater truth was getting into his heart, creating not only hope, but faith. Don't be deceived: faith often requires diligent mental work, often through the help of a caring mentor.

How many times per week are your disciples' minds and emotions trashed, resulting in un-Christlike behavior, ruptured relationships, or damaged influence? They need to bring their hearts to Jesus for restoration, but most don't until they learn how through the help of a discipler. To help them obey, we need to disciple them to guard their hearts (Prov. 4:23).

"If Jesus really cares and is with you to give you what you need, can you go back to school tomorrow?"

"Yes, I can!"

I watched Dave make a tough *heart-choice*, day by day, to go back into his junior high pain. How? He believed he was of infinite importance to Jesus and had a divine mission to accomplish. Imagine being set free by the truth to go back into that terror. But he needed help to get there.

We must help our disciples to authentically embrace their beliefs. Many adults, weary of hearing "Jesus loves me," continue to be ruled by the opinions of others or the longing for approval or the fear of loss of beauty or change in the economy, and so on. They do not sufficiently experience the truth of being personally significant to Jesus. The result is that often they are not confident of being protected and provided for, and with futility they search for value and meaning.

Guiding the heart: "What do you think would be best?"

When the time is right, ask what your disciple thinks about

the situation and what he or she thinks is best to do in light of the situation. This type of questioning looks toward the future, toward action or resolution.

"Pal, what do you think would be the best way of coping with Ryan?"

When I asked Dave about what he thought would be the best thing to do about Ryan, his eyes would usually drop and his countenance would darken. It seemed to me that his pain resulted in an understandable attitude: "Do we have to talk about that?"

Strategically opening my heart: "What do you think I think?"

Instead of telling David what I thought, I often asked, "What do you think I think?"

Suppose your disciple is able to quite accurately communicate his or her thoughts about your thoughts. You could say, "And what do you think about my perspective?" This question is of extreme value for disciplers. Now you can have a meaningful dialogue about whether your disciple agrees with your point of view.

If your disciple does not agree, it is OK. However, you have now earned the right, in essence, to ask, "What are the reasons you don't agree with my perspective?" Your disciple once again has an opportunity in a safe place to sort out life-significant issues while under your guidance, instead of adopting values, attitudes, ideas, and behavior based on cultural influences, temporal desires, or reactions that leave God out.

Asking a question like, "What do you think I think?" is important because it

- maximizes rational discussion while minimizing relational tension
- helps your disciple get outside his or her own perspective and into yours

- tests if your disciple understands your message or perspective
- lessens the likelihood of frustrating your disciple in hearing again from you what he or she already knows you think
- helps your disciple be more open to the next step

Knocking at a heart: Ask permission to share thoughts

Getting permission from your disciples before telling what you think (in the context described here) is like knocking on the doors of their hearts. It gives them the opportunity to open the doors to you, if they desire. It is good training for all relationships. When we kick the doors open by hurling our words at hearts without carefully knocking, they often feel invaded and are not nearly as willing to receive our thoughts. To plant good seed in the soil, we have to work the soil first. Never forget: our motive must be seeking to do what is best for our disciples.

If your disciple says no to your request to share your thoughts, you both know that he or she is closed to you. When you say, "OK, I'll wait till you are ready to talk about it," you didn't get to plant the seed, but you probably made points in the relationship and softened your disciple's heart for a future time. There are emergency times when our disciples need to hear our perspective *immediately*, but not as often as many assume.

Why do adult disciples need the kind of heart-help David needed? What if they appear to have no crisis in life? Why should a discipler intentionally seek to know his or her disciple's story, heart, and understanding of truth? What have you learned in this chapter about heart-probing conversations with your disciples?

Connecting a heart to the heart of Jesus

Now we are into the most important reason for this conversation. As disciplemakers, we diligently seek to bring our disciples to see what Jesus sees. Sometimes I ask what they think Jesus thinks; sometimes I ask permission to tell what I think Jesus thinks.

Let's return to my conversation with David. Once he answered what he thought I was thinking, I was free to tell him my thoughts or raise more questions.

"You know that I try to find out what Jesus says through Scripture. We know that He knows what is best. Jesus loves you and He hates what is happening to you.

"What does Jesus think about the kids at school, including Ryan? How will they figure out that they are important to Jesus? How did Jesus treat His enemies? What could you do to be like Jesus to them?"

As David thought about and answered these questions, God's heart for "loving enemies" was being planted in David's heart. Many of our disciples won't think about loving their enemies without help.

The Spirit of God enabled these questions from Rom. 12:21 to help David establish God's perspective and will. Little seventh grade David, with a giant of a God inside of him, headed into the dreaded halls of the junior high school, ready to return good for evil to his Goliath. David was empowered to obey Jesus.

▶ **My Thoughts**

9 — WALKING WITH JESUS

You continue to walk in truth (2 John 3).

To make Christlike disciples, we help them think with Jesus about their influence

In the last chapter, I shared the miracle of how God's Word and Spirit, working in a battered heart and body, can restore a young disciple. Disciples almost always need a mentor to train them to guard their hearts and walk in truth. The process includes exposing and replacing bad seed in the heart—lies and distortions—with good seed, God's truth. Disciples must be trained to, on their own, "Take captive every thought to make it obedient to Christ" (2 Cor. 10:5).

We continue to investigate question-asking conversations that connect our disciples' hearts with Jesus, preparing them to walk with Jesus.

A serving heart: more than conqueror

Evil did not beat Dave, who had God's truth and power in his heart. First in his heart, then through his life, he conquered rejection and abuse. He was empowered to be more than a conqueror. God and he won the battle for his heart, and then he went into battle for the hearts of his enemies.

I have heard Dave tell the story. "I went back to my school and would say to myself as I walked down the halls, 'Jesus loves me! Jesus loves me! Jesus loves them. Jesus loves Ryan. Jesus calls me to love Ryan.'" Dave was telling himself the truth—God's truth. God was winning the battle for his mind!

The next semester Ryan showed up in five of Dave's classes. Dave kept his commitment to be good and "do good" to Ryan (Acts 10:38). Eventually, good overcame evil. Ryan and Dave became friends. We invited Ryan to our house to stay overnight. In the wee hours of the morning, he asked Dave, "What's up with you? I laughed at you and beat on you, and you turned around and called me 'Friend.'" When Dave told Ryan why he loved his enemies, Ryan wanted to hear more. That night, Dave led his former enemy into an authentic relationship with Jesus. Friends became best friends. They asked the question, "What can we do to change our school?" They started a prayer meeting every morning before school. They found a teacher who would let them use his classroom. They started with five people. Soon they were running twenty, then forty, then sixty. Fifteen years later, between fifty and eighty students were still meeting every morning to study the Bible and pray before school in that same teacher's classroom. That's about 67,000 hours of godly influence.

God's Word plus God's Spirit plus many family meetings and conversations with Jesus allowed David to quickly grow into a man of God, defeating all sorts of giants. The Truth empowered him to not be a slave to the actions and opinions of others.

With Truth dispelling lies, he was free to walk with Jesus and lead others.

Today, Ryan trains missionaries who go to unreached people groups. David is the founder and director of a university prayer and disciplemaking ministry. His recent prayer and fasting conference had over seven thousand students from forty states in attendance. Many others from those morning meetings at the junior high became Christ-followers, including several who became pastors and missionaries. Good can overcome evil. The presence and power of God in a heart can turn despairing hearts into conquering hearts.

Here is the point of this whole story of teaching and leading by asking questions: if our disciples learn to examine and adjust their hearts to equal Jesus' heart, they have power to walk more obediently with Jesus each day. Almost everyone needs great help to develop this necessary skill.

Of all our Christian activities, how important is guarding our hearts and bringing our thoughts to Jesus? Why? How can you help your disciples develop this practice?

Capitalizing on crisis

Disciplemakers do not wish spiritual challenges for their disciples. However, they use challenges as their very best opportunity to train their disciples to talk with Jesus to hear His perspective and to do His will.

Thinking with Jesus

More important than David's battles at school was his learning to think with Jesus—bringing every issue of his heart and life to Jesus for consideration. Had I failed to ask David questions about his heart, I would have abandoned him to thinking on his own—mostly about junior high trauma. The result: feelings of fear, anger, rejection, and experiencing all kinds of godless desires and motives. I shudder to think of the outcome of that junior high battle had David and I not pursued our conversations that included Jesus (2 Tim. 2:16). David needed help to

- slow down
- think with Jesus
- agree with Jesus
- commit to Jesus' will
- be accountable for that commitment

How much is the Holy Spirit quenched and grieved because Christians have not been discipled to stop, think, listen, rethink, believe, and act? Spiritual disciplines must be learned, and they are seldom learned in isolation. They require Christian coaching, practice, reminding, and training. We must have the conversations that help our disciples learn to think with Jesus, not just in the traumas of life, but in day-by-day details so that Jesus is habitually their Leader, not their Follower.

Uniting with Jesus

Because Dave allowed me to listen to his situation, we worked together on the great reason for his being created—real relationship with Jesus. As he answered my questions, he profoundly experienced looking into Jesus' eyes and listening to His voice. What price would you pay for that? Jesus' thoughts became David's thoughts, and Jesus' will became David's will. Authentic, meaningful union occurred, all in David's heart. *It is in the heart that we meet and experience God.* It is possible to unite with God in our hearts—the two can be one (Eph. 5:31-32).

Aided by heart-searching questions, David understood why

he was devastated. But it was in the agreeing and experiencing Jesus' thoughts that David was greatly freed from emotional pain and empowered with significance and purpose. Result: he learned how to cope with all of life's heart challenges, not just the giant ones.

By uniting with Jesus in his heart—agreeing with Jesus about both David and his enemies—David was empowered to unite with Jesus in his life. Instead of being overcome by a battered heart, David was empowered to obediently walk as Jesus walked (1 John 2:3-6).

Loving Jesus

This crisis created the opportunity to establish what I wanted most for David: for him to love Jesus as Jesus loved him (John 17:26). I wanted him to know and feel Jesus' love enough that he would be more responsive to Jesus than to his enemies or me or anyone or anything. Asking questions—not telling—helped this become reality.

Making disciples with Jesus

Because David grew in his ability to know Jesus' heart and was better able to obey Him, he has been able to help his friends, and now his own family and other disciples, do the same. The story unfolds daily how God uses him to preach to thousands and to profoundly disciple dozens, especially his primary disciples, Dawson, Alivia, and Adelyn. He and Renata are intentionally discipling their three children through many meetings, conversations, and questions.

Heart power

Jesus made clear the power of a good heart: "Make a tree good and its fruit will be good, or make a tree bad and its fruit will be bad. . . . The good man brings good things out of the good stored up in him, and the evil man brings evil things out of the evil stored up in him" (Matt. 12:33, 35).

"Above all else, guard your heart, for it is the wellspring of life" (Prov. 4:23).

For better and for worse, hearts determine actions. Disciple-makers must work with their disciples' hearts, training each person to nurture his or her heart above all else.

Heart surgery

The disciplemaker is like a spiritual heart surgeon. He or she must discover what is in the heart, help eliminate what is diseased, and help implant Truth. This frees and empowers disciples to obey.

First, we immerse our disciples in the anesthetic of grace and then open their hearts by listening to stories. Then we ask questions about thoughts, attitudes, feelings, desires, and especially motives.

If we find Christlikeness in the heart, we celebrate. If we find something other than Jesus' heart, we graciously, gently, prayerfully dialogue about it until our disciples genuinely see and agree with Jesus' truth (1 John 1:7-9). When un-Christlike heart conditions are discovered, brought into the light of God's truth, and if the disciple repents of them, darkness normally loses its gripping power. The heart is free to obey Jesus.

Weed seeds—good seeds

This process of discipling a heart is like finding and eliminating the bad seeds that blossomed into un-Christlike behavior, and planting the good seed—God's Word—into an open heart, resulting in good fruit—Christlike behavior.

You might say, "But isn't that the task of the Holy Spirit?"

Yes, to be sure. And He has been absolutely faithful to guide us into truth, to convict us of our sins, to forgive all we have confessed to Him, which we believed He would do. He has not failed. And many of us have responded with all the faith we have. But we, like our disciples, still struggle with human thoughts and attitudes that are not equal to Jesus' thoughts and attitudes (see Phil. 2:5-11) and human motives that are not the same as Jesus' motives (John 5:30). All of Jesus' disciples must learn how to recognize and respond to the voice of the Holy Spirit—to bring every thought captive into obedience to Christ (2 Cor. 10:5). This is not to be about the Holy Spirit *or* the church; it is to be about the Holy Spirit *and* the church. God has created us to need each other and intends that we help each other. He desires that Christians not assume they are so spiritually superior that they need no other Christians.

A heart, even a heart resolved to be fully dependent and devoted to God, can be very deeply entrenched with godless patterns of thinking and unbelief, painful emotions, and naive ignorance of selfish motives. Who can know this heart? The Holy Spirit. But most disciples also need the help of a caring, Christ-following, heart-searching, question asking friend to partner in heart transformation through conversations that include Jesus.

Life trashes good hearts

If we only tell disciples about Jesus' grace and holy call, and leave them with broken hearts, they are like orphans. We are failing Jesus and them. But if we will caringly listen and ask heart-opening questions, we can help bring the trouble into the open. Then, with the help of the Holy Spirit, we and our discipleship partners can often spot which things in our hearts are of God and which are not.[1]

I want to be Jesus' disciple, walking with Him throughout

the day—asking Him questions, bringing troubled thoughts, desires, motives, and emotions before Him, exchanging my heart
for His heart, so that I can say—like He did—"What I did today
is what I heard You asking me to do" (see John 5:19). This requires that I continue to seek truth from my discipleship partners about my story and my heart.

This is essential for becoming like Christ. Far too many people live only by doctrines and rules. They do not talk and walk
with Jesus, by His Spirit. It is my responsibility as a disciplemaker to help my disciples walk in heart relationship with Jesus all
day long. This occurs best through consistent, heart–to-heart
conversations about our stories, our feelings, and Truth himself.

Why ask disciples questions about biblical concepts?

If disciplemakers do not work to discover their disciples'
grasp of truth, and if the disciples can't articulate truth in a safe
environment with their disciplemakers, the disciples can't articulate truth to themselves in life's grind where they desperately
need it. They will feel inadequate to discuss God's truth with
their families. With Christian friends they will be vague at best;
in the workplace, mute.

Conversely, if the disciplemaker asks the disciples to articulate their understandings of God's perspective, they will be empowered to tell themselves the truth they so desperately need in
their battle against their flesh, the world, and the devil. They will
be far better and bolder in raising questions and in discussing
God's perspective with their families. They will become positive
conveyers of God's truth in the church foyer and group meetings. When they have been able to effectively articulate God's
truth to their mentors, they will have courage to ask unbelievers
what they think to be the truth.

To be sure, mentors must teach what Jesus taught. An excellent way to do this is to study straight through a book of Bible, starting with one of the Gospels.

But when will we know that our disciples adequately understand what Jesus taught? For example, when do we know they understand forgiveness? After we have read it in Matt. 6? After we have talked with them about forgiveness several times? No! We won't know that they know until they can sufficiently verbalize what Jesus taught. Disciplemakers must give personal time and attention to allow for this dialogue.

Why ask disciples about their obedience?

Disciplemakers first find out if their disciples know what Jesus has commanded. Next, they find out if their disciples are actually obeying Jesus.

Jesus expects that I teach my disciples to obey all that He taught (Matt. 28:19-20). Is it enough for a parent to tell his or her children to quit arguing and to let the children continue, in spite of what the parent said? No! To teach children to quit arguing, parents must know whether or not the children are consistently, habitually doing what they were told. So it is with our disciples.

You say, "But I don't have any right to do that with other Christians."

Of course you don't, at least not unless you have sufficiently loved them and earned their trust and respect through your genuineness as a Christ-follower—including confessing your own errors to them. Then, when you invite them to meet to help each other know and follow Jesus, they may agree. Then you can say, "Should we honestly report our progress in obeying Jesus each week?" They just might agree. Then you, through your integrity as a Christ-follower, have entered into a mutual relationship of helping each other obey Jesus. You have earned the right and created an environment to mutually share with each other as Jesus did with His disciples (Luke 9:10; 10:17). One of Jesus' commands through His Word is to confess our faults to one another (James 5:16). Further, by sharing with each other you are growing in personally obeying Jesus, who told you to teach others to obey Him.

If the disciplemaker does not ask the disciples what they are going to do with God's Word, and how they did in following it, then the wonderful intentions that flow out of Sunday morning worship experiences, small-group Bible studies, even personal meetings with Jesus often get lost in the old habits and the pressures of life.

An effective disciplemaker helps his or her disciples to commit to specific steps of obedience to God's Word, gets permission to ask for a report at the next meeting, and follows up as planned. For example, this week the men in one of my groups have committed to not disagree with family members until they have asked enough questions to repeat the other's perspective. We will start next week's meeting by reporting our progress. This sets a life-changing process in motion.

- God uniquely empowers the disciple, because both the disciplemaker and the disciples are praying for specific progress in specific steps for obedience.
- The disciples have identified specific steps of action, rather than nebulous "oughts."
- When the disciplemaker verbalizes specific commitments and expects accountability, the disciple is far more likely to remember to obey.
- When discipleship partners come back to the next meeting, meaningful conversation as fellow soldiers in God's army is possible. Either obedience happened or it did not. If it did, there is reason for celebration. If it did not, there

is grace, encouragement, and dialogue about what went wrong, what to do to improve, and so on. Knowing Jesus and following Him are the agenda.

- Dialogue about Jesus increasingly occurs in the informal settings of the family and church because Jesus is becoming far more tangible in the lives of His disciples.
- The disciples' changing lives bless and influence their families, church, and world.

Why ask disciples about their hearts?

Don't forget, it is primarily in the heart that we experience God's presence.

It is in the heart that we exclude Jesus, and sooner or later we suffer, or we include Him and conquer.

If our disciples learn to examine their hearts with Jesus, they can know if they are including or excluding Him. Jesus has thoughts and motives; they have thoughts and motives. If they discover that their thoughts and motives are different from His, they can repent—change their minds—and come into agreement with Him. By doing this, they agree with Jesus. Result: they experience His emotions, and even His desires. When thoughts, motives, emotions, and desires are united with Jesus, these Spirit-enabled, Christlike hearts naturally—supernaturally—have power to do what Jesus wants. And by this we are obeying the Great Commission, teaching our disciples how to obey Jesus all day, every day.

What is this chapter trying to help disciplemakers to do? Disciples?

▶ **My Thoughts**

10 — SERVING LIKE JESUS

Your attitude should be the same as that of Christ Jesus who . . . made himself nothing, taking the very nature of a servant *(Phil. 2:5-7).*

To make Christlike disciples, we disciple them to serve with Jesus

Jesus was a servant.

Jesus' servant lifestyle was demonstrated one night as He washed His disciples' feet. He then clearly commissioned His disciples to follow His servant lifestyle.

> **I have set you an example that you should do as
> I have done for you** *(John 13:15).*

The purpose of this chapter is to establish that Jesus' followers, like Jesus, live as servants of our Father, obediently ministering to others.[1] In order to do this, I recommend the "disciplemaking house church" along with personal coaching. This is different from holding training classes and helping people discover their gifts, which is helpful—even necessary—for some, but seldom sufficient without the relational support and training described below.

Serving others in obedience to Jesus is ministry. Ministry includes fixing cars, preparing Communion, serving on a worship team, and so on. But ministry must mature to include, and to ultimately focus on, relationships and interaction with people. If I truly love my neighbor, I care about more than temporal needs; I care about his or her relationships with God and others.

The disciplemaker establishes his or her disciples in thinking and walking with Jesus. This now expands to helping them obediently serve others. Serving others as Jesus would is part of what it means, according to our analogy in chapter 5, to "baptize" in Jesus' name. So the mentor is now to reproduce in disciples what he or she has previously established as his or her personal way of life.

Paul, inspired by the Spirit of Jesus, punctuates Jesus' call to all Christ-followers: "Your attitude should be the same as that of Christ Jesus who . . . made himself nothing, taking the very nature of a servant" (Phil. 2:5-7).

A new believer, discipled to serve

Joe got up early every morning because he had much to do. While he got ready, he mentally ran through his schedule for the day. He planned quiet time alone to meditate on his newfound faith, the new lessons he was learning through his new faith family, and his dramatic purposes. At breakfast, he read a newspaper to see what was happening in the world. He needed to be able to relate to others in order to lead them from their point of view to his faith. After breakfast, he boarded a train for the commute to work. He took along several magazines that his new leaders had given him. He distributed them on the train seats where others might find them, perhaps read them, and perhaps consider his faith.

He arrived at work early. He wanted his employer and associates to respect him so that they would listen when the time came to share why he was such a good worker. He worked hard until break time. Then he would purposefully connect with other employees, asking about their concerns, needs, and frustrations. He empathized and ministered to them when possible. Through this, he hoped to one day open the opportunity to share his good news about how their lives could be different. He did the same thing at lunch and all afternoon. Every day was filled with meaning and purpose. He desired to lead others into the wonderful life of hope and purpose that he had discovered.

In the evening, Joe would race home to have dinner. He had important work to do after dinner. Some nights, he attended a group led by the leaders of his new faith. Other nights he visited different neighborhoods to serve needy people in any way possible. As he grew in faith, he was asked to mentor new converts. Some nights he joined with others of his faith as they mingled at entertainment or eating locations downtown, seeking to connect with unbelievers in order to share their faith.

By the end of the day, he was exhausted. But he came home with a deep, profound sense of meaning and significance. He had lived every moment of his day on purpose, with purpose, to benefit his community and world. He fell into bed, thinking of what he could do better and how he could passionately, strategically, and purposefully give his life tomorrow to sharing his faith. There was fire in his heart. It was his passion.

So goes the story of Joe. It reflects on a day in his life as a new Communist. Joe's new faith was in Communism. He had seen some Communists ministering—serving others. He listened to their dream and strategy to make the world better. He bought it.

Our Communist friend perceived that he was hearing truth. He believed what he heard. His new faith led him into a new life. Day after day, he lived exactly as I described. He loved Communism and lived every moment for it. He gave four of every seven dollars he made—57 percent—to the spread of his belief that Communism was the answer for the world.

This new Communist learned quickly what Jesus intends every one of His followers to know and practice—full-time ministry. Joe did not quit his "day job" to do the work of the Communist party. Rather, he strategically used his day job to minister as a servant of the party. He used the positive relationships acquired through serving his employer and work associates as a platform to propagate his newly acquired confidence that Communism was the answer to the world's problems.[2]

Did you think Joe the Communist was a new Christian? If so, what did you think about the way he lived as a "Christian"? Do you think Jesus intends that Christians serve Him the way Joe served Communism? What do you think would happen? Why do you think so few Christians serve Jesus as Joe served Communism?

Discipling for ministry

I started a "disciplemaking house church" with Carl and Mary, two brand-new converts from a life of "serious sin." They asked me if I would disciple them. I asked if they would commit to inviting their friends to come to a disciplemaking meeting at their home. They said yes. We started meeting every Tuesday night.

Their disciplemaking process began by opening their home to their many non-Christian friends, inviting each to come and think about Jesus together. Everyone in this group was new to Christianity. Almost every week someone became a follower of Jesus. Each took the biblical message seriously that following Jesus included serving Him wherever they went.

Kristen was one of several who were invited. She came. After hearing about Jesus, she repented, resulting in a transformed lifestyle.

Kristen's husband, Shawn, knew nothing of authentic Christianity—personal or institutional. His perceptions of Jesus were learned on the streets. He was providing for his family and university education by dealing drugs. When Kristen told Shawn that she was attending a Bible study, he rolled his eyes. However, in just a few weeks he was stunned as he watched Jesus transform Kristen's life. Shawn decided to come to Kristen's baptism. Having watched her life and now hearing the conversion stories of others being baptized, Shawn also repented and asked to be baptized.

Why did Shawn radically turn from his old life to following Jesus? Kristen and others fulfilled the first stage in making disciples—"baptizing" (immersing) Shawn, not in water, but in Christlike character, actions, and words. These holy, Christlike acts and words drew Shawn to Christ, repentance, and water baptism.

Now that Shawn had determined to know and follow Jesus, he needed to be systematically and consistently discipled. He was immediately invited to attend the Tuesday night house church.

Note that what happened in that house church was a *group* meeting with Jesus, much the same as the personal meeting with

Jesus described in chapter 6. To be Jesus' disciples requires that we be with Him. To make disciples of Jesus requires that we help others be with Jesus.

It was in this collective meeting *with* Jesus that Shawn repeatedly saw and heard why and how Christ-followers serve with Jesus.

Show

Jesus lived with His disciples. In the process, He demonstrated to His disciples what ministry was about. Every time Jesus' disciples saw Him minister—and there were many—He was effectively discipling them in servant ministry (Matt. 13:10; 15:12; Mark 9:28; Luke 22:39; John 2:11; etc.).

Shawn's peers immediately showed him ministry each week when they reported their successes or struggles in serving Jesus in all their relationships. He easily sensed God's call and provision to serve, for he heard how his new Christ-following friends served Jesus all week long. He was being influenced—discipled—to serve Jesus in all his relationships.

In light of Luke 9:10, what do you think about Christians gathering in supportive groups to report the way they served Jesus in their family, church, and world the preceding week? What benefits and difficulties can you foresee?

By faithfully attending his house church, Shawn was unknowingly preparing to one day serve Jesus by planting his own house church. How? He was observing what to do. By simply being present and unintentionally observing, he was seeing how to make Christlike disciples in a house church setting. More about disciplemaking in house churches later.

Tell

Jesus told His disciples all about ministry before sending them into ministry (Matt. 10:1-42; Mark 4:34; Luke 9:1-6; 10:1-16).

Like Jesus' disciples, Shawn was learning about ministry with Jesus. He was taught

- that all Christians "deny themselves, take up their cross, and follow Jesus"—the One who came not to be served but to serve[3]
- to fix his eyes on Jesus—not on his ability or lack thereof—to effectively minister[4]
- of Jesus' provisions to effectively serve[5]
- that through being sensitive to the Holy Spirit as Jesus was, he could do the very work of Jesus[6]

Shawn believed the Word. He realized that ministry was not about his limitations. Like Peter, his role was to believe Jesus' call and obediently step out of the boat into the challenging waters of ministry, keeping his eyes firmly fixed on Jesus (Matt. 14:22-33). Every week Shawn's house church concluded with a "call to ministry." House church members waited silently for the Holy Spirit to guide them on their walks with Him throughout the coming week. They were then invited to tell their sense of God's

> What do you think about this weekly process for ministry development? Do you agree that much—not all—of ministry is about relating well to Christians and non-Christians? Why or why not?

specific call to ministry. They then prayed for each other, believing their prayers to be according to God's will.

Shawn watched and learned. He was being discipled to serve Jesus with all his heart (Deut. 10:12). Soon, this one who just a couple months ago was very lost, found himself involved in profound Christian ministry. He was learning to follow Jesus, who "went around doing good."[7] He was learning to intentionally "baptize in Jesus' name" wherever he went.

Listen

Jesus listened to His disciples, including giving them opportunity to tell Him about their ministerial experiences.

> **When the apostles returned, they reported to Jesus what they had done** *(Luke 9:10; cf. 10:17).*

As Shawn's house church leader, I attempted to do what Jesus did.

Each week, early in the gathering, I asked the group to give God praise for any progress in serving with Jesus. I usually started by reviewing that every Christian is a member of the Body of Christ. As Jesus did not come to be served but to serve, so all His followers, as His representatives, are to serve others in His name. Thus every week, along with all the other "ministers" in the group, we all *listened* to Shawn tell his story of last week's ministries. The group leaned forward as Shawn reported, clapping with joy and praise to God for all the progress. Shawn assumed that accountability for lay ministry was normal for all Christians, just as it was for Jesus' original disciples.

At the end of the meeting, I consistently asked the group to think about their relationships with family, church, and world, asking Jesus what He may want to do in each relationship. Our meetings were not rushed. I could be quiet and wait. Little by

How much do you think sincere Christ-followers could be influenced to serve through simply experiencing something like what Shawn did in his house church? How much more training do you imagine they normally need? Does anyone help you with gracious and supportive accountability?

little, the group members would verbalize their sense of the Holy Spirit's guidance. We *listened* and rejoiced with each response. Occasionally, if I had questions, I asked for clarification. I listened with great delight to aggressive ministry commitments by new disciple Shawn. I was glad that Shawn was not deceived into believing the lie that only professionals do the ministry.

Next week we would again give praise reports. These reports were positive accountability for what the Spirit had accomplished in partnership with His ministers—those committed to serving Him wherever they were.

Quite regularly there would be reports of missed opportunities to minister, or failed attempts. The group reacted to the disappointing reports sometimes with encouragement, sometimes with weeping. This became the perfect environment to listen and learn about ministry, not only "out there" in life, but "in here" with the Body of Christ. Why? House church members asked questions, listened, encouraged, prayed, and helped each other listen to the Holy Spirit or Scripture. Sometimes members of this ministry team confessed that they had behaved in ungodly, sometimes horrendous ways. The listening, sensitive hearts of the house church ministered grace to the disgraced and courage to the discouraged. (Professional pastors desperately need this kind of supportive, disciplemaking group.) They celebrated honesty, affirmed God's grace and mercy, and talked together about how ministers of Jesus respond to these "ministerial" errors. Then, out we would go for another week of ministry. It was a good school of ministry. We felt like soldiers in a battle worthy of our lives. We were.

Shawn assumed it was normal Christianity. He was right. He was maturing as a nonprofessional but highly effective minister.

Watch

Jesus watched His disciples. Once He asked them about their argument regarding greatness (Mark 9:33-37). This illustrates that for three years, Jesus' disciples were under the watchful eye of the Servant. He watched and coached their attitudes about serving.

Noting Shawn's willingness to serve, I invited him to join me in ministry to others. My twofold purpose was to strengthen his ministry skills by allowing him to watch me but more importantly by allowing me to watch Shawn. The process generally followed this pattern: Shawn would watch for a few times. Then Shawn would lead the ministry experience as I watched. For Shawn, this was mostly as I helped him plant his own house church. Somewhat for Shawn, and much more for others, ministry observation included

- personal appointments with house church members to listen and help each grow as followers of Jesus.
- friendship evangelism experiences with pre-Christian friends. Sometimes it was influencing them at a ball game. Often it was having lunch—being sensitive for the opportunity of leading his friends toward Jesus.
- known emergencies in the house church, including visiting the hospitalized.
- identifying problems in the house church, then prayerfully seeking and implementing solutions.

• facilitating disciplemaking house church meetings with Jesus.

After watching Shawn minister, I was able to affirm that the Holy Spirit had helped and used him. If Shawn was struggling as he ministered, I could discern whether to jump in and help or to let him work through the process, knowing help was available. Regardless, after each experience, I would ask Shawn what he thought went well, what needed improvement, and how to improve. Shawn was getting very good ministerial training. He was becoming an effective minister. Through this process he was learning how he would later disciple others to be ministers.

What good comes from observing "ministers in training"? Why might it be worth the time of a busy Christian leader—lay or professional—to watch a minister in training?

Review

In Shawn's house church, week after week, we talked about Jesus. We reported good things Jesus helped us with that week. We talked to Jesus, thanking and praising Him. We confessed our errors. Week after week we learned from the Word, His Spirit, and each other. We talked about how we believed Jesus wanted to serve through us that week, resulting in prayer and commitments. We came back week after week, reporting what we had experienced as we walked with Jesus. We built relationships centered on Jesus and being His disciples, thus serving Him in all our relationships. Everyone who came was taught and believed that Jesus called him or her to follow Him in ministry. It was every pastor's dream.

Ministry equipping

Because of the presence of the Holy Spirit, almost every Christian has significant potential to minister. Certainly, every Christian has the right—and most have the need—to expect their church to provide ministry equipping (Eph. 4:11-12) and discipling (Matt. 28:18-20). Without the Spirit, Shawn cannot minister. Without the church to disciple him, Shawn probably will not minister.

Note God's Word for church leaders:

> **It was he who gave some to be apostles, some to be prophets, some to be evangelists, and some to be pastors and teachers, to prepare God's people for works of service, so that the body of Christ may be built up** *(Eph. 4:11-12).*

The leaders of the church are to *prepare* God's people for ministry. But well-intended leaders have often been deceived. We have often assumed that teaching, preaching, seminars, books, and so on, provide sufficient preparation. We have confused teaching and training. Teaching is a necessary first component in discipling. But it is not sufficient. Jesus dramatically demonstrated this. He prepared His followers by selecting a few to intensively disciple for ministry. He did more than teach—He modeled, listened, watched, and coached. He even took them into His most difficult experiences to let them watch Him fight for faith. He discipled them.

Based on this chapter, describe the disciplemaker's role in ministry training, then the disciple's role. Why and how do you fit into both roles?

God's people—all of them—are to be equipped for ministry. Church leaders can inform thousands at a time. To *form* ministers requires discipling a few who will in turn be empowered to disciple others for ministry.

The next three chapters tackle the greatest challenges of the Great Commission: "teaching them to obey *everything*." Please proceed prayerfully.

▶ **My Thoughts**

11 --- HOLY LIKE JESUS

But just as he who called you is holy, so be holy in all you do *(1 Pet. 1:15).*

To make Christlike disciples, we must help our disciples be holy, for Jesus was holy

What does this holiness look like?

There is a legend about a man who was the most powerful king in the world. The reason for his control over all other kingdoms was his superior army with its superior horses. His horse trainers had learned superior ways to train horses. In the midst of battle, with clashing of swords and the agonizing screams of warriors, these horses were trained to remain sensitive to their riders' commands and nudges. In the distraction, noise, and pain of battle, these well-trained horses could not be distracted. At any cost, they had to listen for and be obedient to their riders.

After preliminary training, a final test was given to see which horse would be selected for the king himself. This horse had to be the best of the best. Many were equally strong, equally fast, and equally trained. But the horse for the king had to have the ultimate loyalty for the king—obedience at any cost.

The king's horse had to learn to respond to many signals. One signal was a particular whistle. This whistle meant that the horse was to instantly come to the king, no matter the obstacles.

The best horses were trained and given this final test. A corral was built on the side of a ravine. The river that cut the ravine was splashing along a few hundred feet downhill from the corral. The fastest, smartest, strongest, best trained horses were led into the corral. The gate was shut.

The horses were given no food or water for a day. They were hungry, but far worse was their thirst. They could see and smell the water in the river just down the hill from the corral. They scouted every section of fence, searching for a way of escape.

A second day came and went with no food or water. The horses were famished, but that was small compared to the scream of their bodies to quench the thirst. Desperately needing water, they pawed at the corral, attempting to beat down the sides to escape.

The third day was the same. No food, no water. Now dehydrated, these best of the best horses were losing their fight. They had spent all their energy seeking release from captivity. They were broken. Hope for living was dying.

Then, during the third day, the trainers opened the gate. The barrier was gone. The life-giving, life-saving water was within reach. Hope, then energy, returned. It was downhill all the way to the water. The horses bolted through the opening, down the hill, gravity serving them in their mad dash to life.

Suddenly, while running at top speed, halfway down the hill, a trainer blew the king's whistle. This whistle meant "come to the king, no matter what the obstacle." Instinctively, upon hearing this whistle, the horses halted their mad dash to the river. For a bone-jarring moment they responded, caught between their desperate need for water and the months of training to come to the king's whistle. But only for a moment. Almost all of the horses succumbed to their body's scream for water. They ignored the whistle and satisfied their own needs.

But every once in a while a horse more noble would hear the whistle and oppose the downward momentum. This horse would painfully turn, mustering every available source of energy to respond to the whistle. This horse would deny himself, even to the point of death. This horse was selected for special service—to be the special servant of the king.

Do we hear the whistle of our King? A thousand legitimate thirsts will scream at us to rush downhill. Many of our friends, some of our heroes, will be heading toward the river. And it is understandable if one loses sight of the big battle and our King. There is always enough logic in taking care of our own thirsts that it makes good sense to ignore the whistle of our King and continue downhill. Our friends will call us to be reasonable and join them in satisfying legitimate appetites.

But every once in a while, every so often, someone more noble hears the whistle of our King. This one denies himself or herself, takes up whatever cross, battles through every obstacle necessary, to follow this King—to respond to His whistle. That servant, that soldier, will be of special service to the King. Is your devotion to your King pure? Have you heard His whistle?

The secret of those who respond to our God's whistle while battling through every kind of need and seducing desire is love and love alone. Love is the only force more powerful than the rumbling of our own appetites and the cries of our earthly thirsts. This love begins not with our own love for God but with the knowing and experience of His love for us—we love because He first loved us (1 John 4:19).

If we desire to hear and respond wholeheartedly when God blows His whistle, we will take care to cultivate the awareness of His great love in our own hearts and in the hearts of those we are mentoring. Aware of His affections, our hearts are alight with love for Him. Empowered by this love, we will listen for and hear His voice, and our hearts will respond even if it costs us greatly.

Think with me about the following connection between the Great Commission and the Great Commandment.

Jesus' Great Commission to His disciplemakers is most demanding: "Teach [your disciples] to obey everything I have commanded." Everything? Isn't that kind of overwhelming? Where do we start? What would it look like?

Here is a hopeful starting point. To teach our disciples to obey everything Jesus commanded, we might logically start with what Jesus identified as the first and greatest commandment: "Love the Lord your God with all your heart and with all your soul and with all your mind" (Matt. 22:37).

Then, when our disciples love Jesus wholeheartedly, they will be on course to obey all His commands (everything), for Jesus said, "If you love me, you will obey what I command" (John 14:15).

Their food—energy and enjoyment—will be to do the will

> Do you think that many capable, well-trained Christians often give in to their earthly thirsts instead of denying themselves for their King? What do you think Jesus thinks? Do you think He sees that they simply do not have their hearts set on fire by the flaming fuel of His love?

of God (4:34). Add ongoing discipling plus the Holy Spirit's help to this wholehearted devotion, and obedience to all of Jesus' commandments will follow.

Disciplemakers are to teach other similar commands: "Be holy" (1 Pet. 1:15); "Be perfect" (Matt. 5:48).

Holiness of heart, perfect love, entire sanctification, and pure devotion are similar phrases describing the Great Commandment.[1]

What can we do to help our disciples establish holy, radical resolve to love and follow Jesus with all their hearts?

Pray for pure devotion

Jesus prayed for His disciples to be sanctified, and so we pray similarly (John 17:17). It is in answer to prayer that God promises to sanctify us and our disciples (1 Thess. 5:23-24).

Satan deceives us into a lack of discipline in our prayers for Christlikeness. He knows that if a sizable core of Jesus' Church loves God wholeheartedly, then righteousness, divine power, and an evangelism explosion will rock the world. God joyously answers our desperate prayers for pure devotion to counteract the relentless spiritual war Satan wages against our pure devotion.

What should we pray *for* (and *with*) our disciples?

- To be delivered and protected from evil (Matt. 6:13; John 17:15)
- For cleansed and purified hearts (Acts 15:8-9; 2 Cor. 11:2-3)
- To be filled to the fullness of the Father, Son, and Holy Spirit (Eph. 1:23; 3:19; 4:13; 5:18)
- To be sanctified (John 17:17; 1 Thess. 5:23)
- To be one with Jesus and the Father (John 17:11)
- To be perfect and mature (Col. 4:12)

Demonstrate pure devotion

Our disciples deserve to see us as fully devoted people; they *need* to see it. Seeing true passion for Jesus in the lives of others creates hunger for personal passion for Him.

Continual awareness of divine love is the key to pure devotion. If my love grows cold, it is much easier for me, like the well-trained horses, to rationalize my "need for water"—be it more food and sleep; or a better house, car, or wardrobe; or approval from others; or something else. On the other hand, when my mind is filled with the gripping awareness of Jesus' immense love, devotion for Him fills my heart. Then I find myself longing to offer everything to Him. The first offering: keeping my heart close to His.

I pray that my disciples see in me pure devotion to Jesus, demonstrated first by spending time with Him. I pray they see that I have compassionate love for everyone, evidenced by obediently giving myself to people and things that best accomplish God's will. I pray they see great vision, optimism, peace, joy, and Spirit-empowerment as the fruit of faith in my great King. I pray they see Jesus guiding and empowering every act, word, decision, minute, and dime. When I become aware of my failure to demonstrate any of the above expressions of wholeheartedness, I must confess to everyone affected.

Why is it a priority to pray for Christlikeness—personally and for others? Will you do this? Who will hold you accountable by asking you if you are praying for Christlikeness?

Teach to obey everything, including pure devotion

God desires and asks us to give ourselves fully to Him, and the

Bible tells us He is a jealous God. Many people rightly teach the love and grace of God but then fail to announce that a nominal or neutral response to His holy love leads, at best, to excruciating pain in the Lover. God does not invite us to anything that He himself has not greatly exceeded. His heart hurts when we do not respond to Him fully, largely because as we respond with all our hearts, we enter into the delights for which He created us and the joy of mutual fellowship with Him for which He gave everything.

"Jesus' timeless call for the entirety of the human heart is aimed directly at this yearning He placed in us. His charge is issued out of the truth of love's nature—love's demand for all and its refusal of half-heartedness."[2]

Twenty-eight biblical reasons for pure devotion are referenced below without explanation. All of them communicate God's real expectations—and His will—that we be entirely devoted to Him. Because these are God's expectations, disciple-makers are radically resolved to help their disciples

- seek God with all their hearts—Jer. 29:13; 2 Chron. 15:12; 22:9; Ps. 119:2, 10, 58
- return to God with all their hearts—1 Sam. 7:3; 1 Kings 8:48; 2 Chron. 6:38; Joel 2:12
- trust God with all their hearts—Prov. 3:5
- praise God with all their hearts—Pss. 111:1; 138:1
- serve God with all their hearts—Deut. 10:12; 11:13; Josh. 22:5; 1 Sam. 12:20, 24
- obey God with all their hearts—2 Kings 23:3; 2 Chron. 34:31; Ps. 119:34, 69
- ultimately, love God with all their hearts, souls, minds, and strength—Matt. 22:37; Mark 12:30; Luke 10:27; Deut. 6:5; 13:3; 30:6

In light of the Bible's call to pure devotion, and our call to teach our disciples to obey everything, dare we do less than

- help our disciples joyously walk by faith in God, believing that He is doing His part to make pure devotion possible (1 Thess. 4:3; 5:23-24)?

- encourage our disciples to perpetually consecrate themselves fully to God (2 Chron. 16:9; Rom. 12:1-2)?

I do not teach these commands of the Bible as legal demands. If they were, they would not come from a source of love. I treat them as greatly desired relational expectations. These commands are possible as a by-product of knowing Him, whom we love because He first loved us. When we truly know His love, we are pained by doing less (1 John 4:19).

Love's expectations may not be required, but when unfulfilled, Love himself is greatly hurt. I do not want to peer into Jesus' eyes on Judgment Day, realizing that He and I both know that I gave myself mostly to pleasure, money, and things, when He received only a fragment of my heart (2 Tim. 3:1-5).

Nor do I want to look back on life and realize that I could have discipled my family and others to love Jesus with all their hearts, but I simply ignored it.

I urge my disciples to set their will to live entirely for Jesus and His purposes, a commitment made possible by God's desire that we be fully His. Through prayer and determination, God makes our love mature over time. If Jesus had given in to the anguish He felt in Gethsemane, He may not have embraced the Cross. But He chose the Cross because He was committed to doing His Father's will and could see the joy that would come later (Heb. 12:2).

> How would you try to help someone love Jesus so much that he or she would lay down his or her life—each day's activities—for Him? Do you love Jesus like this?

Crosses hurt. We never *feel* like taking up our cross. But when we take up our cross, our willpower is spurred on with the joy-generating vision of what will result. Thus we follow Jesus, even against the pressures of our flesh and culture.

Starting the fire

How can our disciples abandon every idol to sacrifice their whole lives, even suffer, for Jesus? Answer: when they draw near to the passionate heart of Jesus, their hearts catch fire (1 John 4:9, 19; Rom. 12:1-2; 2 Cor. 5:15)! When they begin to understand the depths of His love, their hearts will be compelled by the same thing that compelled His first disciples. They will abandon themselves to God and find their hearts saying with Paul, "I consider everything a loss compared to the surpassing greatness of knowing Christ Jesus my Lord" (Phil. 3:8).

When our disciples clearly grasp this Heart that
- created them for a love relationship
- breaks with each act of their indifference
- chose not to retaliate but to mercifully suffer
- rejoiced over their initial response to grace
- savors each of their present responses to Him
- desires and invites a wholehearted response, greatly for their sake
- delightfully anticipates reigning and ruling with them forever

then our disciples will be greatly strengthened to love wholeheartedly.

Sustaining the fire

We sustain our desire to completely commit to God through new and renewed revelations of God's love that started the fire. The fire of pure devotion is primarily lit and sustained at Jesus' feet. As we consistently meditate on Jesus' passionate love, the Holy Spirit ignites our bored, lukewarm, divided hearts with passion for Jesus. This is the way we must meet with Jesus—alone, in worship settings, and with holy comrades.

> **Let us purify ourselves from everything that
> contaminates body and spirit, perfecting holiness
> out of reverence for God** *(2 Cor. 7:1).*

When the fire of passion burns low, perfecting holiness is minimized. To make Christlike disciples, I must help my disciples understand why and how to keep their fires of devotion burning brightly. The "how" happens primarily in beholding Jesus' devotion for everyone (John 15:9).

Dialogue the distinctions between a divided and a pure heart

Our disciples need a clear message that contrasts a divided heart and a pure heart.

> **But mark this: There will be terrible times in the
> last days. People will be lovers of themselves, lovers
> of money . . . not lovers of the good . . . lovers of
> pleasure rather than lovers of God—having a form
> of godliness but denying its power** *(2 Tim. 3:1-5).*

Note that these folks all have a form of godliness—probably call themselves Christian, attend church fairly regularly, even have positions in the church. Note the various objects of love: self, money, pleasure. Note that the great commandment to love God with all their hearts is consistently broken; they have several other lovers.

Deep down, many view pure devotion to God as eccentric or mystical or extreme (Christlikeness is quite narrow [Matt. 7:13-14]). They view the great commandment as purely optional, at best. They seem to think that it is perfectly healthy, balanced, and appropriate for Jesus to be merely one piece of their life's pie. They believe they can love things: pleasure, money, significance, security, and success, and give themselves essentially and primarily to these. And, oh, yes, they believe they can also love Jesus and make Him a 5 to 10 percent piece of the money, time, loyalty, and conversations of their life's pie. One consequence of giving Jesus only 10 percent of our lives: we will not enter the joy and delight of the very love relationship for which we were created.

Imagine how troubled we are when we find out that a husband has been cheating on his wife. Suppose he only cheats one night a year? We hardly see this as acceptable.

What about our relationship with God? God truly intends that His people not be spiritual adulterers (Hos. 1:2). He sees the heart, and oh what He sees. He is truly jealous and notes well when we depend on and devote ourselves to anything rivaling Him.

Simultaneously, His delight is great as we seek and respond to Him in any area. He delights boundlessly when we allow love to do that which is its very nature to do—to take over our whole lives and not just parts.

Jesus died to have a pure, spotless bride (Eph. 5:25-32). Is it too much to say that the nominality and lukewarmness of the Church has become so normal that we don't bat an eye at a divided, spiritually adulterous heart, and that we assume that anyone who is entirely devoted to Jesus is in the very least being extreme?

What is the solution? Our disciples must grow in understanding the incomprehensible love of God (Eph. 3:18-19).

Dialogue with disciples about our Father's pure devotion

God is infinitely devoted to everything that empowers pure

devotion for Him. What could be written about our Father's ungraspable love that has not been explored? He so loves people the rest of us would never dare to love that He would request His own Son become a lasting sacrifice to create eternal relationship for all who would respond. Oh, that our repentant disciples who have responded to our Father's love can experience the depths of His heartfelt joy in them. Beyond heartfelt joy, God's heart explodes with passionate delights and pleasures when His children look to Him for guidance and help. His delight and pleasure is magnified and multiplied when we mature enough to authentically care about Him and His desires.

Please think carefully with me as I try to help us feel the fiery passions of our Father's love. Our Father's holy, righteous, passionate love has been trivialized by our failure to observe His jealousy as a component of His love. Our hearts are moved when we experience the infinite devotion of God's heart. Our hearts also profit from the fear that occurs when we realize God's jealousy regarding choices we've made with indifference to Him.

I, the LORD your God, am a jealous God
(Exod. 20:5).

Do not worship any other god, for the LORD,
whose name is Jealous, is a jealous God *(34:14).*

As the lover of our souls, God observes every nuance of our hearts. He experiences every movement of each heart toward Him but also every movement—dependence or devotion—to anything other than Him. Dependence on anything other than Him is idolatry. The intensity of His delight when our attitudes or actions are motivated by Him is countered by His utter abhorrence—jealousy—when we are motivated by anything or anyone other than Him. When God sees our hearts looking elsewhere, He feels our neglect and abandonment. It is truly offensive to Him.

Remember, God perfectly sees and delights in the heart that wills His will, regardless of maturity level. Suppose God's Spirit shows me a particular pleasure that captures my heart more than Him. Suppose that upon realizing this heart condition, I honestly desire change and seek help to change. Jesus says, "Perfect!" Progress in love will come through a heart resolved to love.

As painful as it is for our holy God to experience our idolatries, it is more painful for Him to abandon us in our idolatries. Why? The core of His heart is compassionate love as witnessed in the sacrifice of His Son's life.

When our disciples grasp our Father's wholehearted devotion, they will better grasp His hatred of sin's divisions and destructions. Then they can better appreciate the pain in His heart while He mercifully, gently confronts our sin, desiring that none perish. Talk about our Father's love that sentenced His Son to die for us! In awe, we will spend eternity discovering the magnitude of what the Father gave in the giving of His Son for us. How could one not love this Lover?

Dialogue with disciples about Jesus' pure devotion

In His last hours, Jesus suffered great anguish. But His devotion to His Father strengthened His resolve. Selfless compassion for every person who does not know God, including His enemies, motivated Him. His anticipation of eternity with a sanctified Church—loving Him as He loves it, thinking what He thinks, feeling what He feels, wanting what He wants—invigorated Him (Heb. 12:2). Think how Jesus must have loved every person so much that He gave up His equality with God to embrace the human suffering that freed us! To suffer indescribably for all people!

> I am jealous for you with a godly jealousy.
> I promised you to one husband, to Christ, so that
> I might present you as a pure virgin to him. But I
> am afraid that just as Eve was deceived by the
> serpent's cunning, your minds may somehow be
> led astray from your sincere and pure devotion
> to Christ *(2 Cor. 11:2-3)*.

What is the motivating truth that will draw our disciples to be filled to the fullness of God? Answer: grasping and knowing the love of Jesus. We must "see" Jesus (Eph. 3:18-19; note John 12:21; 14:31; 15:13; Eph. 5:25-32).

Talk with your disciples about the Holy Spirit's pure devotion

We don't see heart-idolatry the same way God sees it. The Spirit of grace is also the Spirit of truth and holiness. I wonder if the following overstates or understates the holy passions of the Spirit of holiness:

He loves us to the full extent we ever conceive of being loved by Jesus, or our Father. He demonstrates this love, in part, by burying himself deeply in our willing though badly divided hearts.

It was one thing for Jesus to live among sinners. It is an altogether different thing for the Spirit of holiness to enter into redeemed hearts that are ignorant of idolatrous divisions. There He dwells, sees, hears, smells, and touches idols which are unspeakably repugnant to Holiness himself. He immerses himself, laboring in our unholy, idol-saturated attitudes, desires, and motives. He knows—we usually don't—when Jesus is merely one of our many lovers. He graciously exposes this idolatry—for our sake, for Jesus' sake, for everyone's sake. He experiences our neg-lect—even rejection—of His counsel, but stays on. He is quenched and grieved, but doesn't leave. Holiness himself, whose eyes are too pure to look on sin, has salted himself into sin-blinded hearts to convict and cleanse. He surely longs for free-dom from this stench-of-sin, impure environment as much as Je-sus did the Cross. But compelled by love, and communicating love, He heroically stays, patiently exposing idols. He devotedly works, exposing and eliminating false lovers who contest His supreme passion—glorifying the magnificent Christ that Christ alone would reign supremely as the object of our full dependence and devotion (see John 16:14; Col. 1:19).

Coach pure devotion

God has never been negligent in answering our prayers for holiness, and most of those prayers have been sincere. However, we are suffering a crisis of pure devotion. Why? There certainly needs to be clear preaching and a lot of prayer for holy hearts and lives. There are other culprits, but a great one is our failure to graciously and openly talk together about complete devotion. Wesley said, "There is no holiness but social holiness." A Wesley scholar recently told me that Wesley meant Christians cannot sustain and mature in wholeheartedness without Christ-centered conversations plus accountability.

> I am afraid that . . . your minds may somehow
> be led astray from your sincere and pure
> devotion to Christ *(2 Cor. 11:3)*.

> Let us consider how we may spur one another on
> toward love and good deeds *(Heb. 10:24)*.

By living a purely devoted life, I learn some of its challenges. What I learn in maintaining pure, fiery love for Jesus becomes God's gift, by which I can graciously, wisely talk with my disciples about wholeheartedness.

Wholeheartedness normally requires caring conversations to positively stay the course without negatively judging others, self, or God.

Mentors desiring to help their disciples love Jesus wholeheartedly need to invest special time in these disciples, asking questions like these:

Why is it essential for fully devoted disciples to consistently talk with their discipleship partners about pure devotion to Jesus?

- Are we making progress in being sensitive to Jesus before we make decisions, speak, and act?
- Are we dialoguing with Jesus about our thoughts, attitudes, and motives?
- What does Jesus think about our progress? Our intentions?
- Is pure passion for Jesus in place? If not, are we wholeheartedly resolved to love Jesus? If not, what can we do?

The Holy Spirit makes holiness possible. It is a matter, first, of the heart. God judges the heart. When we resolve to be holy, our performance improves, and God calls it perfect.

▶ **My Thoughts**

12 ⸺ MAKING CHRISTLIKE DISCIPLES

Obey everything I have commanded you *(Matt. 28:20)*.

Go and make disciples *(Matt. 28:19)*.

To make Christlike disciples, we must help our disciples make disciples

Disciples who serve can and must be discipled into disciple-makers who lead.

In the Early Church, every Christ-follower was called a disciple of Jesus. These disciples were not called Christians until someone gave them that nickname in Antioch (Acts 11:26). Only two other references occur where Jesus' movement or followers are referred to as Christian. Both are in the context of the Roman government who opposed them for claiming someone other than Caesar was Lord. One is by the Roman King Agrippa, who wonders if Paul is seeking to convert him to being one of the Christians (Acts 26:28). The other is Peter writing to Jesus' disciples, reminding them that they may suffer at the hands of the Romans for being "Christian" (1 Pet. 4:16).

On the other hand, well over 200 times in the New Testament Jesus' followers were called His disciples. Like most words, the meaning of being a disciple got lost with time and use. But originally, everyone knew and understood that a disciple was someone who was invited into a very serious personal relationship with a rabbi or mentor or master. The DNA of the movement Jesus started and the method He commanded for its multiplying assumed intensive, personal mentoring for every person in the movement.

What will it require for God to restore us to His original intent? Disciplemakers! We cannot be discipled without disciplemakers. A disciplemaker is a "spiritual parent" who adopts a manageable number of "spiritual children," including their biological children, to intentionally and strategically "baptize each in Jesus' name." They love, listen, and then lovingly lead each to obey everything Jesus taught.

Family or orphanage

The church is intended to function like a family. In a healthy family, good parents give personal attention and affection. They give clear direction about what is intended and what is forbidden, because parental love does what is best for the children. Good parents not only expect obedience with their caring directives but also inspect their children's responses, giving promised rewards for compliance or disobedience.

The church has generally been more like an orphanage than a family. The orphanage-type church does not have the caring, personal relationships needed to establish obedience. On Sunday morning the director of an orphanage-type church announces the directions. The well-intentioned but immature spiritual orphans nod in agreement or raise their hands or even come forward for prayer, vowing to obey this week's directions. But, in an orphanage with a hundred orphans and only one director, it is nearly impossible for the director to know what all the orphans did that week or why or be able to graciously help each little one to understand his or her battle and how to do better this week.

The next week, the orphanage director stands up and delivers more orders on another topic. Many of the poor little orphans did not want to come to the meeting because they had so badly failed to obey last week's orders. However, they mustered up enough courage to come. But no one—including the director—asked them what they had done the last week. Some were disappointed because they really wanted help. Others were relieved because they did not want to be embarrassed in front of all the other orphans. Now, new orders were coming. The people all gritted their teeth, vowing to do better this week.

The next Sunday, it all happened again. Guilt-ridden orphans reluctantly trudged back to the big meeting room for more directions. Their experience was repeated, and then again the next week and the next, and on it went. Often the orphans were divided into groups to talk about what the director said but never to find out if anyone did what the director said.

Gradually, a perception began to form in their minds. They concluded that it really was not too important that they do what the director had been saying, though it would be nice. What really mattered was that they come to hear each week's new directions. So, feeling relieved, they came to listen to the director to receive new, unique, intriguing, inspiring insights every week. It got to the place that if he repeated himself, some grumbled. Some even looked for another orphanage.

Jesus must be sad that there are so many orphans. He expects every one of His followers to be personally and sensitively cared for by a spiritual parent-disciplemaker, including being taught to obey everything Jesus commanded. Teaching to obey does not mean to shout directions, though God expects His Word to be plainly taught. Teaching to obey works best in the context of close and lengthy relationships: real caring, real knowing, real wisdom. It works best in Christlike discipling relationships.

How realistic is the orphanage scenario? How many spiritual parents—disciplemakers—would it take to adopt and disciple 100 spiritual orphans?

From pagan to disciplemaker

Following Jesus' disciplemaking outline in Matt. 28:19-20, we will trace a new disciple's journey from conversion to making disciples.

Going and baptizing

Larry had just remarried. His new stepson, a fairly new convert, baptized—immersed—Larry in Jesus' name. He didn't lightly sprinkle him; he drenched him. He physically threw open his arms to embrace his new stepfather every time possible. He blessed him with gifts and invitations to events, sincerely caring for him. It wasn't long until stepson invited new stepfather to visit our church.

Larry came. He was an outgoing, energetic former marine. I asked permission to meet with him and his wife. He invited me to their home. After several times together, both he and his wife responded to Christ's invitation to follow Him as Savior and Leader of their lives. He told the church his story at his water baptism.

Teaching

Larry faithfully sat on the third row during our Sunday worship services. He also started coming to one of the house churches I led. In these venues, he learned a whole new way of seeing and living life. He learned how to personally meet with Jesus in the house church. In order to be discipled as much as possible by Jesus, we challenged him to meet with and learn from Jesus on his own, just as we did it in the house church. He did. He was being discipled—by Jesus' Spirit, Word, and church.

Teaching to obey

Each week in the house church, Larry watched and listened to others share, not just their ideas, but their lives and ministry. He learned that being a disciple of Jesus is about doing, not just believing (James 2:17). He listened to stories of progress. He listened to stories of struggles. He joined in, including making commitments each week to what Jesus was leading him to do that week. He was being taught to obey.

Through Scripture, good examples, and focused teaching, Larry committed to what Jesus' disciples do: meet with Jesus consistently (alone, small group, and large group) and minister with Jesus constantly (family, church, and community). Larry loved to help, and in no time he was aggressively serving Jesus' church. He joined the worship team. He built displays and helped clean the church in emergencies. He fixed cars for those with financial needs.

Simultaneously, he struggled with habits and relational tensions. By honestly reporting his successes and struggles, Larry steadily matured in Christlikeness.

Teaching to obey everything

Larry was F.A.S.T.: Faithful, Available, Submitted to Jesus, and Teachable. He did not have to unlearn a truckload of old theologies and traditions. What he saw and heard, he asked about until he was clear. It often took a long time for him to articulate clearly. But when he got it, he put it into practice.

As Larry's mentor it was not enough for me to be satisfied that he was doing well as a minister. For me to obey Jesus, I had to teach Larry to obey everything Jesus taught. This included helping him with heart holiness.

But it included more.

Until my disciples are obeying Jesus' command to make disciples, I have not yet taught them to obey everything. This is a time-consuming, difficult step omitted in some schools of discipleship, trivialized in some others.

I had helped Larry commit to nonprofessional but full-time ministry, being good and doing good everywhere. Remember that this ministry is the *informal* first step in disciplemaking.

Now, I had to intentionally help him to proactively and effectively make disciples.

One way to make disciplemakers: plant disciplemaking house churches

Within weeks, I encouraged Larry to gather his family members and friends—those he had been "baptizing"—to meet with him and me at his house. If he would, we could start another disciplemaking ministry. I told him that if he was willing to gather people in his house, I would lead the meeting for a while, modeling disciplemaking practices. He could help by participating actively but also learn by watching. Then I would incrementally have him lead the meeting, coaching as long as necessary. In this way I would disciple him to make disciples in the house church setting. He was willing.

Before tracking further with Larry's progress, it's important for you to know what my "open" meetings for disciples and "closed" meetings for disciplemakers are like.

Open meetings for disciples

I invite everyone to my house churches. These meetings are open to anyone with no conditions. In open meetings, I seek to make disciples of Jesus as described in chapters 6 and 10. This includes challenging them to start their own house churches, like Larry in this chapter.

In my open meetings, there are three important strategies that distinguish an intentional disciplemaking meeting from more casual groups. Each strategy is an integral component of "Meeting with Jesus."

1. *Understanding.* The disciplemaker intentionally asks disciples questions to see if disciples understand biblical issues well enough to both explain them and explain why these issues are important. Those who cannot articulate truth and its importance in this supportive environment will find it difficult to tell themselves the truth on their own. Examples: "Can you explain 'grace' so that a seven-year-old can understand you?" "What do you mean by 'shed blood'?" "Why is that important?"

2. *Commitment.* The disciplemaker secures commitment from group members to specific action steps (ministry, obedience) to be taken in loving God and neighbors (starting with family) during the week.

3. *Accountability.* Early in the next meeting the disciplemaker asks for a praise report of God's help. This is constructive accountability.

Closed meetings for disciplemakers

Among the Twelve, Jesus gave intensive attention to Peter,

James, and John.[1] My "Peter, James, and John" are those who are actually involved in Jesus' commission to make disciples. I give specialized attention to these disciplemakers, including inviting them to my closed meetings. To be invited to this meeting, one must be formally making disciples by leading at least one weekly disciplemaking meeting for his or her family and/or friends.

Facilitating closed meetings for disciplemakers

I seek to regularly meet with ten to twelve disciplemakers, either personally or in closed meetings for disciplemakers only. I seek to help my group in both making disciples, then making disciplemakers.

At this writing, I regularly facilitate four closed meetings for disciplemakers. The purpose of our meetings is to encourage and equip disciplemakers.

Meeting process:

- Disciplemakers' praise to God, especially reports of progress in disciplemaking.
- Disciplemakers' questions and challenges, with the group helping each other toward solutions:
  - Personal challenges—those committed to making disciples face increasing time pressures, possible increase in tensions or criticisms (they are seeking to lead others), and probably increased demonic attack. They must be growing in Christlikeness, often a major topic.
  - Challenges regarding disciples and disciplemaking.
  - Biblical, theological, and methodological challenges.
- Biblical, theological, lifestyle, or disciplemaking concerns I raise.
- Prayer for progress.

One-on-one closed meetings are best; more than four or five in a group meeting dilute the process. Due to the great needs of fledgling disciplemakers, I normally invite each to a closed group for disciplemakers plus one-on-one meetings.

In our congregation, everyone who is gathering family or friends for a weekly open meeting with Jesus for disciples is invited to closed meetings for disciplemakers.

Securing necessary time with disciples and disciplemakers is one of the greatest challenges. The key is to understand precisely what actually needs to be accomplished, and then be creatively flexible in structures—both relational disciplemaking structures and congregational structures—to accomplish what is needed to make disciples who make disciples.

Back to Larry. Because he was willing to make disciples using a disciplemaking house church, I committed to meet with him personally.

Each week before his family and friends gathered at his house to meet with Jesus, Larry and I would meet for one hour. I aggressively asked him questions about

- biblical materials he had agreed to study[2]
- last week's ministry, especially to his new disciples
- any questions or concerns about being and making disciples of Jesus
- what he planned to do at this week's meeting

We worked on how to help others understand, commit, and report. In no time, Larry was effectively discipling new converts he had invited to his house to meet with Jesus together. The very things I had helped him understand and put into practice, he effectively helped his disciples to know and do (2 Tim. 2:2). After just a few months of personal meetings, Larry was profoundly obeying Jesus' Great Commission to make disciples.

Like Jesus, we must call our disciples to make disciples. We must teach them to obey all of Jesus' commands, including make disciples. Anyone unwilling to try to make disciples might be resisting Jesus' Great Commission and may thus have a disobedient heart (Matt. 28:20). Our disciples may resist particular disciplemaking strategies; they must be helped to embrace Jesus' command.

How long do we disciple disciplemakers?

How long do parents work with children? My children's greatest challenges may be their children. If they are interested, their parents might be the ones to help them with parenting, since grandparents have considerably more experience in parenting than new parents.

The same is true of disciplemakers. I intend to disciple my disciplemakers (think Larry) *as long as they desire help* in making disciples who make disciples. If my disciplemaker discontinues the process for whatever reason, the work we have already accomplished will bear fruit, and I will be free to invest in another disciplemaker.

We move now to the final—and absolutely necessary—step: multiplying disciplemakers. This requires God's power, our great faith, love, patience, and long-term *relationships.*

▸ **My Thoughts**

13 — MAKING CHRISTLIKE DISCIPLEMAKERS

All authority in heaven and on earth has been given to me . . . I am
with you always, to the very end of the age *(Matt. 28:18, 20).*

To make Christlike disciples, we must help our disciples make disciplemakers

Christlike disciples make disciplemakers, for Jesus made disciplemakers.

Imagine the Father saying to disciples, "How pleased I am with you. And I am overcome with joy that you are helping others to be My Son's disciples. You are even getting them started in making disciples. You are calling them to pray for specific persons to come one step closer to Me. You are helping them to immerse these specific persons in grace, pouring kindness into their lives, and sprinkling invitations to meet with Me. I am so very pleased with you.

"But there is one more giant hurdle. It is not like My Son's cross, but it may feel like it to you.

"Now, call them to plant a house church, just like the one they attend at your house. Help them to gather family and friends to meet with My Son there just as they do at your house. Help them to teach their disciples to obey, not just a few rules, but to obey as My Son did, walking sensitively to My Spirit and seeking to do nothing apart from Me. And help them to help their house church attendees to understand what it means to be holy as I am holy.

"All you did with your disciples, you can help them do with their disciples—including this final crucial step: help them make disciples. They need more help from you in this than anything else you have done with them. It is your last big hurdle—making disciples who make disciples.

"Pray for your disciples now more than ever. Stay as close as necessary to listen, not only to their relationship with Me, but to how they are doing in helping others walk with Me. This is the key to multiplication and massive evangelism. Set up regular meetings as much as necessary to pray and give them help.

"You are so close. If My Church ever realizes that almost everyone can parent spiritually, and does it, a wonderful explosion of salvation and righteousness will occur. Go for it. Don't quit now. Lead the way. Help your disciples obey Me by making disciples."

A maker of disciplemakers

One of the best makers of disciplemakers in our congregation is Ruth. Her story could inspire anyone to make and multiply disciples. She is quiet and not what most would call a natural leader, but her disciples are intentionally making disciples. Her ministry focuses on helping her disciples persevere and grow in disciplemaking.

Ruth moved here seven years ago and secured a job. She supervised the care of nearly one hundred senior adults at a care center. But Ruth understood that she worked with and for Jesus, "baptizing" everyone, everywhere, all the time with His love. She worked her forty or more hours per week at the care center with excellence. She let her light shine, and others saw her good deeds and praised her Father in heaven (Matt. 5:16). That was her fourth priority.

In her "spare" time, Ruth lived by her first three priorities.

1. *Be discipled by Jesus.* Ruth gets up very early every morning to meet alone with Jesus. She then makes her way to a 6:30 A.M. group meeting with Jesus that meets every weekday morning. For seven years, the only times she missed were for vacations, work and witness mission trips, and one sick day. That is about 1,750 hours being discipled by God's Word, Spirit, and people, plus that many personal meetings with Jesus. She did her best to spend several hours every Saturday alone with Jesus, plus two or three services every Sunday in worship and educational experiences. Her love and faith reveal that she has been with Jesus (Acts 4:13).

2. *Make disciples in the family.* Ruth's six children are all grown. She faithfully prays for each, plus her ten grandchildren. She welcomes all to her home. She "baptizes" them with excellence, writing, calling, visiting, serving, and listening. She asks if there is interest in pursuing Jesus' perspective regarding challenges.

3. *Make disciples in the church.* She methodically connects with women in and out of the church, "baptizing" them

with kindness, interest, invitations to coffee or lunch, and invitations to be a part of her house church to meet with Jesus together. It meets at 7 P.M. every Tuesday night. If Christmas Eve came on a Tuesday night, and it was ten below zero, I imagine Ruth would encourage everyone to do what they should, but remind them that she would be there, with coffee on and ready to open the door. She has invited well over one hundred women. Approximately thirty have come at one time or another, being encouraged and discipled to know and follow Jesus. This little church that God empowered Ruth to plant and pastor meets in her two-bedroom apartment. Women have gone back to their families converted, better, stronger, and able to influence their families and worlds. But this is just the beginning.

Teaching disciples to obey everything: make disciples

Ruth is navigating the challenges of the final level of making disciples: her disciples are becoming disciplemakers. She is helping them. She gives more time helping her disciples make disciples than she gave helping them be disciples. Making leaders is more challenging than making followers.

Ruth is helping her ladies make disciples the way she did. What she has done is what Jesus commanded in Matt. 28:19-20.

- *Going and baptizing in Jesus' name.* Ruth commissions her ladies to bring Jesus' grace and blessing into the life of everyone possible, but to focus on a specific few. Each of them has experienced this through Ruth, so they understand its value and have seen it modeled. Most of her house church attendees have now begun this foundational step of informally but intentionally making disciples.

- *Teaching.* Ruth persistently encourages all her ladies to invite everyone possible to a meeting with Jesus at their own homes or other location, just like she did with them. She consistently invites others to the services of our church, again modeling for her disciples what they can do to lead others.

Melody is one of Ruth's disciples who is now a disciplemaker. Some of those Melody is "baptizing" have started to attend her house church. Any who come to Melody's house church will be helped to meet with Jesus, just as Melody learned to do each Tuesday at Ruth's house.

It took a couple years, but first one, then two, and now eight of Ruth's disciples—house church attendees—have each planted her own house church. Ruth's disciples are making disciples. Ruth is making disciplemakers. Others are noticing.

All of Ruth's disciples who planted their own house church need and receive special attention from Ruth. She intentionally works with each of them, not just as disciples of Jesus but as disciplemakers with Jesus. Not as followers but as leaders. These are the ones Ruth invites to her meeting for *disciplemakers* on Saturday mornings. This meeting is closed to all except those who are formally making disciples. These are Ruth's long-term disciples.

How does Ruth know what to do at her meeting with her disciplemakers? Every Tuesday after work she attended a meeting for disciplemakers, led by her mentor, closed to all but disciplemakers. There she observed how to lead her meeting for disciplemakers, and there she raised any question she had in making disciples and disciplemakers.

We all know the challenges of raising a family or pastoring a church. Ruth is pastoring a church on Tuesday night. On Saturday mornings she meets with all her disciplemakers to help them with their house churches. This is a major task. She spends a lot of time beyond the group meeting for disciplemakers, listening to her disciplemakers privately to encourage and equip them as they make disciples in their house churches.

- *Teaching to obey.* Ruth has trained her disciplemakers not only to lead a house church but also to obey from the heart. Her disciplemakers have experienced long conversations about their own obedience, and they are progressively helping their disciples to be doers of the Word, not hearers only.

Some of Ruth's mentors don't have enough time to pastor their own house church, plus attend Ruth's Tuesday night house church, plus attend Ruth's Saturday morning meeting for disciplemakers. Ruth encourages these people to leave her Tuesday night house church and to meet her on Saturday morning where the emphasis is on helping disciplemakers. She assures them that any personal questions or challenges that might normally be raised at the Tuesday night house church can also be raised at the disciplemakers' meeting on Saturday or in a personal meeting.

- *Teaching to obey everything.* When Ruth helps her mentors influence their disciples to make disciples by planting house churches, Ruth has successfully raised her disciples to full maturity. Her joy and thanksgiving should know no bounds.

By God's grace, Ruth will have made disciples who matured into disciplemakers and whose disciples matured into disciplemakers. Everyone is growing up! This is very uncommon but not unintended by Jesus.

What is the dream?

Counting all the groups led by Ruth and her disciples, people are meeting with Jesus an average of one hundred fifty hours per week. Ruth's prayer and vision is to so disciple her ladies—about ten of them—that they are Christlike wherever they are, that they intentionally disciple their families plus ten more ladies to grow in Christlikeness, resulting in one hundred forces for good in families, churches, and the world. She intends to help her ten to each help ten to mature into disciplemakers, so that one thousand people are being influenced through her life in the next ten years.

Parents are better prepared to help their grown children as parents than they were able to parent their own children. Why? They have twenty-plus years of parenting experience. Once Christ-followers are making disciples, they have the experience necessary to help their maturing disciples make disciples. Thus they make not only disciples but also *disciplemakers.*

Training leaders is more demanding than training followers. For as many years as necessary, my disciples—and yours—desperately need a good spiritual parent who will help them in leading their own spiritual children. Raising spiritual children is very hard and inconvenient work. None of us, including our disciples, unintentionally wander into successfully accomplishing difficult tasks. In every arena of difficult endeavor, we must be taught, trained, coached, and discipled. Our greatest task as disciplemakers is persevering with our disciples, helping them mature as disciplemakers.

Obediently making disciplemakers is Jesus' directive to bring His life and eternity-transforming gospel to every group of people on the planet. If I disciple ten to disciple ten who disciple ten, I will have helped to plant one thousand little house churches that minister to ten thousand people. This process will multiply, for it will be experienced and perceived as normal Christianity, which it is.

(Note: If my disciples, or their disciples, ever feel that they are simply a part of someone's dream or vision—a cog in the machinery—they legitimately question what is occurring. Everything Jesus did was motivated by perfect love, and making disciples must always be motivated first by the disciplemaker's love for Jesus, then love for his or her disciples—not primarily the accomplishment of a worthy vision.)

What if we don't help our disciples become disciplemakers?

If I fail to help my disciples make disciples, a few—very few—might intentionally determine to make disciples. The Word and Spirit of God that already captures the heart of intentional disciplemakers are still speaking clearly.

But the raw fact is this: the vast majority of Christendom is traumatized—nearly paralyzed—by the thought of intentionally adopting even a born-again Christian to parent to maturity. The worries of life, the deceitfulness of wealth, and the desires for things (Mark 4:19) have been more than sufficient to rationalize our failing to invest time in adopting and raising spiritual orphans. By the Word and Spirit alone, most have not and will not set out to intentionally make disciples. If I fail to challenge, encourage, and coach my spiritual children to raise spiritual children, it doesn't happen.

The following two paragraphs are not about success, they are about *persistence* in *attempting* to obey Jesus. Michael Jordan missed many, many shots, but he did not quit shooting.

If our disciples are willing and seeking to make disciples, we celebrate with them. But if our disciples are *unwilling* to attempt to make disciples (note the heart component), they might have a disobedient heart regarding Jesus' Great Commission. Further, if they are unwilling to try, they are ultimately disobedient to the Great Commandment, for Jesus said that if we love Him, we will obey Him (John 14:15). We do not want to leave our spiritual children in a place of disobedience to the Great Commandment and the Great Commission.

If you and I are *unwilling* to attempt to help our disciples to make disciples, we ourselves have disobedient hearts to both of the great callings. As righteous and noble as it is for us to make disciples, if we do not complete the task by helping our disciples to make disciples, we fail to teach them to obey everything Jesus commanded, for we are commanded to teach them to make disciples. Through this disobedience to our Great Commissioner, we disobey our Great Commander, for we are demonstrating our lack of love to Jesus himself (John 14:15).

With God, nothing is impossible

But this is all so possible! We are so close! We must not stop before our disciples are committed to being disciplemakers. Our Father is nearly shouting, "Don't quit before finishing the task. You are so close. Lead your disciples to make disciples."

What is the hope for success for those sincerely committed to teaching others to obey everything—including teaching them to obey the command to make disciples?

The first component of the Great Commission gives every reason to expect success:

> **All authority in heaven and earth has been
> given to me** *(Matt. 28:18).*

The last component of the Great Commission gives every reason to expect success:

> **I am with you always, to the very end of the age**
> *(v. 20).*

The Spirit of God is present to release power in response to our prayer and obedience. What is impossible with humans is absolutely possible with God (Matt. 19:26). The One who calls us lives in us to equip, enable, and empower us to

- be Christlike disciples of Jesus
- make Christlike disciples of Jesus
- make Christlike disciplemakers

He has all authority, and as we obey Him, His power is perfectly available to implement His authority. As we trust and obey Jesus, He will actually strengthen our hearts while influencing those we pray for and seek to disciple.

If God is for us, who can be against us?
(Rom. 8:31).

The one who calls you is faithful, and he will do it
(1 Thess. 5:24).

**I can do everything through him who
gives me strength** *(Phil. 4:13).*

In making disciples, Jesus will be with us, always! God is on our side. Our faith is not in our knowledge, our zeal, or our ability. This is not nearly so much about us as it is about God. We must not quench God's Spirit by believing it is impossible and so not do it. With God, all things are possible.

Where from here?

- Has the Lord spoken to you through this book? If so, can you write His message to you? What is your response to Him? (Don't make excuses or blame others; rather, establish holy resolve to be discipled and make disciples.)
- I pray you have or will find one or more discipleship partners with whom to partner in personal Christlikeness, keeping in mind Jesus' relationship with His Father, His character, and His ministry.

- If you live with or in proximity to family, I pray you will engage them as your discipleship partners/disciples.
- If you do not presently facilitate a disciplemaking-type group, could you invite everyone possible and start? If it would help, you could invite potential attendees to read this book to see if they are interested. Consider personally inviting parents or small-group leaders who are interested in being discipled in order to disciple their families or groups.
- I recommend not starting with sermons, fanfare, all-church programs, or other activities. Just invitations. If you are concerned about feelings of favoritism, invite everyone through written or public invitations. If too many for one group respond, start and lead as many groups as necessary.
- Over time you will be able to determine who to invest in long-term.

Conclusion

Do you remember the story of the horses from chapter 11? If you don't, consider reading it again. Let me repeat the questions at the end of the story.

Can you hear the whistle of the King, our King? A thousand legitimate thirsts to be satisfied will scream at us to rush downhill. Many of our friends, even some of our heroes, will be heading full speed to the river. And it is understandable if one loses sight of our King and His battle for every heart. Somewhere there is enough truth in taking care of our own earthly needs that it makes very good sense to ignore the whistle of our King and continue downhill. Our friends, by their lives and words, will call us to be reasonable and join them in satisfying legitimate pressures, even needs.

But every once in a while, every so often, someone hears the whistle of our King and denies himself or herself and takes up whatever cross, gives up whatever's necessary, battles through every obstacle necessary, to follow our King, to respond to His whistle. That servant, that soldier, will be of special service to the King in the great war being waged to free every captive from eternal tyranny. Do you think Jesus knew what He was doing? Do you think Jesus knew what He was talking about? Do you hear His whistle?

Based on the Great Commission of Matt. 28:18-20, can you explain why normal Christianity intends that all be discipled to make disciples and disciplemakers? Will you explain this to others? Who? When? Are you, with God's help, sufficiently discipled to make disciples? Disciplemakers? If not, will you commit to the Lord to securing help from Him and others until you are effectively making disciples and disciplemakers? Will you ask some authentic Christians to hold you accountable for your progress in making disciplemakers?

▸ **My Thoughts**

_____

_____

_____

_____

_____

NOTES

Preface

1. For information, contact office@gvnaz.org.

Chapter 2: History's Most Empowering Relationship

1. The author's personal conviction is that Jesus, while never abdicating or losing His full divinity, truly became flesh, was one with us and truly one of us, emptying himself of the knowledge and use of His supernatural abilities as God, becoming like us in every way, even being tempted in every way like we are. If Jesus' incarnation included any dimension of supernatural ability of which we are devoid, He had advantages we do not have, He really was not like us, He was not tempted as we are, nor could He serve authentically as our representative. Through authentic incarnation, what Jesus did of a supernatural nature He did by the presence and power of the Holy Spirit, through sensitivity, faith, and obedience to His Father. This conviction, though far from universal, is also far from unique to the author. Agreement is not necessary to validate what follows. However, if correct, Jesus' example in being discipled exposes the desperate need for all to be discipled (Phil. 2:5-9; Heb. 2:17; 4:15; Luke 2:52; 3:22; 4:1, 14, 18; 10:21; John 1:14; 5:19, 30; 7:17; 8:29; Acts 2:22; 10:37-38).

Chapter 3: Making the Most with Less

1. Matt. 4:24; 8:14; 9:35-38; Luke 7:36-50; 14:1; 15:2-5; 18:15-17; John 2; 4—6; 9; etc.

2. Matt. 5—7; 23—25; Luke 12:1-59; 16:1-18; 17:1-10; 22:37; 18:1-8; 20:45-47.

3. Matt. 13:10, 36; 15:12; 17:10, 19; 19:23-30; 26:1-2; Mark 4:34; Luke 8:9; 10:23.

4. Matt. 26:36-46; Luke 9:18; 11:1; 22:39; John 17:1—18:1.

5. Matt. 8:23; 9:19; 12:1; 14:22; 15:21; 17:25; 20:17, 29; Mark 6:1; John 11:7-44.

6. Matt. 9:10; 15:32-38; Mark 14:22; John 13; 21:12.

7. Luke 10:38-42; John 2:2-11.

8. Matt. 17:1-13; 28:16-20; Mark 3:7; 6:31; 7:17; John 11:54; Mark 6:31; 9:30-31; Luke 9:18; John 2:12; 3:22; 6:3; 11:7.

9. Matt. 8:25; 9:37; 12:49; 14:15-21, 26-32; 26:6-13; Luke 9:46-48, 55; 21:5-36; 22:24; 16:13; 18:1; 26:31-35; Mark 8:33; John 4; 12:4-8; 20:24-29; Matt. 16:24; Luke 14:25-35; John 12:24-26; 15:13-15.

10. Hal Perkins, *If Jesus Were a Parent*, 194-95.

11. Matt. 16:24; Luke 14:25-36; John 12:24-26; 15:13-15.

Chapter 4: Is Making Disciples Optional?

1. Douglas Hyde, *Dedication and Leadership* (Notre Dame, Ind.: University of Notre Dame Press, 1977).

2. Communism failed because of its godless vision and morality, and ultimately because God himself opposed the movement. This does not diminish the fact that Communism flourished, because many of its strategies to convert and mature its converts were precisely those Jesus practiced and commanded His Church to follow.

3. For rationale of this statement, see author's book *If Jesus Were a Parent*.

4. The problem with Sunday School classrooms: we can't build enough classrooms to house what Jesus wants to do. We already have homes planted all over our cities precisely in the neighborhoods of those we are called to love and reach—our neighbors. Why not have little house churches—Houses of Prayer everywhere—planted in every neighborhood of our cities?

5. Obedience will be examined theologically in chapter 7.

Chapter 5: Step One for Everyone

1. Dallas Willard, *Renovation of the Heart* (New York: Harper Collins Publishers, 2006), 240, 267.

Chapter 6: Learning from Jesus

1. Charles Shaver, *Basic Bible Studies* (Kansas City: Beacon Hill Press of Kansas City, 1972).

2. For Encounter information, contact Craig Rench at craig@a1naz.com.

3. Leaders listening to learners is a primary component in two of the author's books: *Leadership Multiplication* and *If Jesus Were a Parent.*

4. *Leadership Multiplication* is an interactive, question asking/answering Bible study of 33 core theological and methodological topics from a Wesleyan perspective. For information, contact office@gvnaz.org.

5. More detailed explanations for meeting with Jesus are included in the author's books: *Leadership Multiplication, If Jesus Were a Parent,* and *Meeting with Jesus.*

Chapter 8: Thinking with Jesus
1. Gen. 6:5; Deut. 4:9.
2. Exod. 4:14; Lev. 19:17.
3. Gen. 34:3; Exod. 35:21.
4. 1 Chron. 28:9; 1 Cor. 4:5.
5. Exod. 7:14; 35:21; Deut. 8:2.

Chapter 9: Walking with Jesus
1. Because the Holy Spirit is with us, we are not left alone as orphans (John 14:17-19). But most need great help in learning sensitivity and responsiveness to the Holy Spirit.

Chapter 10: Serving like Jesus
1. Throughout this chapter, "serve" and "minister" are used interchangeably, coming from the same Greek word.
2. Hyde, *Dedication and Leadership,* 22-24.
3. Matt. 10:38; 16:24; Mark 10:35-45; John 13:15; Phil. 2:5-11; 1 Pet. 2:20-21.
4. Matt. 19:26; 21:21-22; Mark 9:23; Eph. 3:16-21; Phil. 4:13; 2 Cor. 12:9-10.
5. Rom. 5:5; Acts 1:8; 1 Pet. 4:10-11; Rom. 12:6-8; 1 Cor. 12:1-11.
6. Matt. 10:19-20; John 14:10-14; 16:7, 13-15.
7. Acts 10:38.

Chapter 11: Holy like Jesus
1. Theological technicalities regarding this pure and perfect love relationship are beyond the scope of this book; authentic sanctification is essential to the process of Christlike disciplemaking.
2. Dana Candler, *Entirety* (www.danacandler.com), 20.

Chapter 12: Making Christlike Disciples
1. To assist laypersons incapable of attending seminary or Bible school, I use my *Leadership Multiplication.*
2. Matt. 17:1; Mark 5:37; 14:33; Luke 8:51; 9:28.

RESOURCES

Bonhoeffer, Dietrich. *The Cost of Discipleship.* New York: Simon & Schuster, 1995.

Coleman, Robert E. *The Master Plan of Evangelism.* Grand Rapids: Baker Book House Co., 2003.

Extreme Devotion. Nashville: W Publishing Group, 2001.

Frangipane, Francis. *Holiness, Truth and the Presence of God.* Cedar Rapids, Iowa: Arrow Publications, 2005.

Grubb, Norman P. *Rees Howells Intercessor.* Amsterdam, Netherlands: Holland-Breumelhof N.V., 1967.

_____. *Touching the Invisible.* Fort Washington, Pa.: Christian Literature Crusade, 1989.

Henderson, D. Michael. *John Wesley's Class Meeting: A Model for Making Disciples.* Nappanee, Ind.: Evangelical Publishing House, 1997.

_____. *One Conversation at a Time.* Kansas City: Beacon Hill Press of Kansas City, 2007.

Kreider, Larry. *The Cry for Spiritual Fathers and Mothers.* Ephrata, Pa.: House to House Publications, 2000.

Making Disciples of Oral Learners. Bangalore, India: International Orality Network, 2005.

Malloy, Rocky J. *G-12 Groups of Twelve: Launching Your Ministry into Explosive Growth.* Tulsa: Impact Productions, 2002.

Nysewander, Mark. *No More Spectators: The 8 Life-Changing Values of Disciple Makers.* Kent, England: Sovereign World Ltd., 2005.

Perkins, Hal. *If Jesus Were a Parent: Coaching Your Child to Follow Jesus.* Hal Perkins, 2006.

_____. *Leadership Multiplication.* Kansas City: Beacon Hill Press of Kansas City, 1983.

_____. *Meeting with Jesus.* Kansas City: Beacon Hill Press of Kansas City, 1978.

Virkler, Mark and Patti. *Dialogue with God: Opening the Door to 2-Way Prayer.* South Plainfield, N.J.: Bridge Publishing, Inc., 1986.

Willard, Dallas. *The Divine Conspiracy: Rediscovering Our Hidden Life in God.* New York: HarperCollins Publishers, 1998.

_____. *Renovation of the Heart: Putting On the Character of Christ.* Colorado Springs, Colo.: NavPress, 2002.

Wynkoop, Mildred Bangs. *A Theology of Love: The Dynamic of Wesleyanism.* Kansas City: Beacon Hill Press of Kansas City, 1972.

Yohannan, K. P. *The Road to Reality: Coming Home to Jesus from the Unreal World.* Altamonte Springs, Fla.: Creation House, 1988.